D1328447

THE CENTERS OF CIVILIZATION SERIES

FEZ

In the Age of the Marinides

Fez

IN THE AGE OF THE MARINIDES

ROGER LE TOURNEAU

Translated from the French by
Besse Alberta Clement

NORMAN: UNIVERSITY OF OKLAHOMA PRESS

Books by Roger Le Tourneau

Fès avant le Protectorat, S. M. L. E. Casablanca, 1949.

L'Islam contemporain, Ed. Inter-Nationales. Paris, 1950.

Damas de 1075 à 1154, Imprimerie Catholique. Beirut, 1952.

Les débuts de la dynastie sa'dienne, La Maison des Livres. Algiers, 1954.

Les villes musulmanes d'Afrique du Nord, La Maison des Livres. Algiers, 1957.

Fez in the Age of the Marinides. Norman, 1961

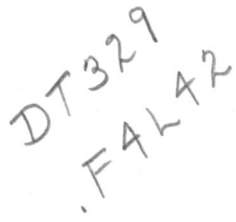

Library of Congress Catalog Card Number: 61–6496

Copyright 1961 by the University of Oklahoma Press, Publishing Division of the University.
Composed and Printed at Norman, Oklahoma, U.S.A., by the University of Oklahoma Press.
First Edition.

To the memory of the late Professor Lévi-Provençal

INTRODUCTION

IN THE MIDDLE OF THE FOURTEENTH CENTURY, Fez was one of the most important Moslem cities. Within Morocco itself, Marrakech no longer possessed its former prestige; it had ceased to be the capital of the country a century earlier. Tlemcen, conquered by the Moroccans after lengthy wars, had been incorporated into their empire in 1337. Tunis remained the capital of a dynasty of Moroccan origin which, though powerful in the thirteenth century, had undergone a serious eclipse in the fourteenth. Damascus and Baghdad had suffered cruelly from the Mongolian invasion in the thirteenth century and were licking their wounds. With the exception of Granada, the Moslem cities of Spain had all become Christian in the thirteenth century. Granada, however, remained in unstable equilibrium between the threatening Christians and the covetous Moroccans. It was more the symbol of a Moslem Spain that refused to die than a true Moslem city sustained by a great state. Only Cairo of the Mamelukes could, in the middle of the fourteenth century, lay claim to greater importance than Fez.

Fez was at the time not merely the capital of the apparently stable kingdom of the Marinides; it was also an important center of commerce maintaining business relations with Mediterranean Europe, with the Arabian East, and with the black country across the Sahara. It was, in addition, a city of learning and religion where numerous students devoted themselves to the study of the Arabic tongue and Islamic science; where writers distinguished themselves in poetry, history, theology and juridical speculation; where, beside the orthodox scholars, flourished mystics who maintained in the city an intense spiritual flame. The proof that Fez did not owe its fortune solely to the success of the Marinide sovereigns may be found in its situation during their long period of decadence. Even after they were replaced by the weak Wattasides, who were destined to wield their power only in the northern half of Morocco, the city did not cease to exist, or even to prosper. The descriptions of it given to us in the sixteenth century by authors as various as Leo Africanus, Marmol, and Canon Clenardus bear irrefutable testimony to this fact.

The Marinides had chosen Fez for their capital as soon as their power was firmly rooted, beginning about the middle of the thirteenth century. But, involved in frequent wars with their neighbors, who were attempting to overpower their nascent state, and with the Christians of Spain, who were harassing the Moslems of the peninsula, they could not immediately devote all their efforts to the development of their chosen city. It was thus only little by little, after the Marinide warriors had conquered their adversaries and had been able to turn their attention to works of peace, that their capital reached its full brilliance.

Moreover, slow development was characteristic of Fez, not only under the Marinides, but throughout its whole preceding history. Certain Moslem cities blossomed forth suddenly, like desert flowers after a heavy rain. Almost from the beginning, Baghdad and Cairo, created to be capitals of great empires, rose to the requirements of their roles and immediately became opulent cities. Other Moslem cities, such as Damascus, Aleppo, and Mecca, were the inheritors of a long past. Fez did not belong to either of these two categories. It seems to have been established by Moslems in a place where no important human settlement had ever existed. It experienced a difficult adolescence and grew slowly in the course of centuries. In order to better understand the situation of Fez under the Marinides, it is necessary to review briefly this long past. It will be seen from what human elements the city was gradually formed, and how it reached its full bloom in the fourteenth century.

CONTENTS

FEZ

In the Age of the Marinides

I

FOUNDATION AND EARLY HISTORY

It is indeed surprising that no settlement was made at the site of Fez until the end of the eighth century A. D., for nature seemed to have marked there the location of a city. With good reason, the advantages of this site have been pointed out by many authors, from the Arab chroniclers of the Marinide epoch to the scholars of our time.

Fez stands at the crossroads of two great channels of communication determined by features of the terrain. One goes from the Mediterranean (Tangier, Ceuta or Peñon de Vélez, the ancient Badis) to the Sahara, and beyond, into the black country, crossing the plain of Saïs, on whose edge Fez is located; the Middle Atlas, whose lowest pass (6,200 feet) is situated just to the south of Fez; the valley of the Moulouya; and the range of the High Atlas at the pass of Telghemt (6,200 feet). Farther on, this route follows the valley of the Wad Ziz to the oasis of Tafilalet. Overall it is nearly straight-lined and is passable even in winter, for in the mountainous regions that it crosses the snowfall is not abundant. The second route goes from the Atlantic Ocean to central Maghreb, now called Algeria. Its path may vary between the ocean and Fez, but, from there on, it is fixed by the terrain. In order to reach Taza, the only relatively easy point of passage toward the East, the traveler must follow the valley of the Wad Fez, cross that of the Sebou, and penetrate into that of the Inaouene,

Marinide Palace

Leper House

Bab Gisa

Bab Sidi Bu Jida

FORMER ALMOHADE QASBA

Madrasat al-'Attarin

Jami' al-Qarawiyin

Madrasa Misbahya

Bab Khukha

Bab Mahruq

Madrasat as-Saffarin

Bu Khareb

Jami' al-Andalus

Marinide Gardens

SUBURBS

Madrasa Bu Inaniya

MADINA

Madrasat as-Sahrij & Madrasat as-Sba'iyin

Bab as-Sba'

Bu Jlud

Wad

Bab Ftuh

Bab Bu Jat

RABAD AN-NSARA

Bab al-Hadid

Wad Masmuda

Bab al-Hamra

Wad Fez

Jami' al-Kabir

AL MADINAT AL-BAYDA   FEZ JDID

Lalla Ghriba

Jami' Az-Zhar

Jami' al-Hamra

Bab Jdid

Bab Semmarin

Bab Jiaf

LAUNDRYMEN

HIMS

Wad az-Zitun

0   500   1000   2000   3000 feet

FEZ AT THE TIME OF THE MARINIDES

which will lead him to the Taza gap and, on the other side, to the smoother ground of eastern Morocco. Fez is thus located at the intersection of two great arteries of communication. It must be noted, however, that the one that led to the south was for a long time a blind alley, since commerce with the black countries did not develop until use of the camel permitted regular crossings of the Sahara—that is to say, not before the fifth century of our era. This probably explains why the Romans neglected the site of Fez: the southern route was of no use to them, and it is not at all certain that their provinces of Mauretania Cæsariensis (Orania) and of Mauretania Tingitana (northern Morocco) were ever connected by a road. At the time of their domination, the site of Fez was not located at a true crossroads.

The situation of Fez presents another advantage of considerable importance in Maghreb: water is abundant there. In fact, the water absorbed by the calcareous formations of the neighboring Middle Atlas constitutes an immense subterranean water table which gives rise, in the Saïs plain, to multiple springs whose junction forms the river, or rather, the rivers of Fez. In addition, other springs gush forth on the steep slopes of the little valley hollowed out by the Wad Fez. Therefore, even if an enemy besieging Fez succeeds in diverting the course of the river temporarily, as has actually happened, the inhabitants are not completely deprived of water, since it wells up even within their walls. It may be added finally that the city was built in close proximity to quarries which furnished construction materials, not far from the forests of the Middle Atlas and their immense reserves of wood, and was located in the center of an arable and fertile region.

In spite of all these advantages, it appears that no important human establishment occupied the site of Fez before the end of the eighth century A.D. The Arab chroniclers assert that, although there were no remains at the time when the Moslem city was founded, an earlier city had existed in that location. No text, Latin or other, no archaeological discovery up to the present time, confirms anything on this subject. Even admitting the supposition that it had sheltered a human establishment in ancient times, it may be presumed that at the late date of the eighth century the small valley of Fez was filled with underbrush and wild animals and served as hunting and fishing grounds for certain Berber tribes.

At the end of the eighth century A.D., an Arab named Idris ibn-Abd Allah, a descendant of the Prophet Mohammed, was obliged to flee into exile from the East, where his family was persecuted by the famous Caliph Harun al-Rashid. He sought refuge in Further Maghreb (Morocco) which, some fifty years earlier, had shaken off the yoke of the Caliphs. A Berber tribe welcomed him, recognized his authority, and permitted him to create a Moslem state which appears to have grown rapidly. Such progress was made that Harun al-Rashid heard of it, took umbrage at it, and sent to Further Maghreb an emissary charged with poisoning Idris. The mission was carried out. However, Idris left a Berber concubine pregnant with his child; two months after his death she gave birth to a son who, in his turn, received the name of Idris. He was reared with solicitude by the Berbers who had brought his father into power, and by an Arab freedman wholly devoted to the descendants of the Prophet. The child grew, reached a precocious maturity, and, according to tradition, in 808 A.D., at barely sixteen years of age, already possessed the ability to continue the work left unfinished by his father.

There are two conflicting traditions associated with these events concerning the founding of Fez. According to the better known one, recorded by comparatively recent authors (thirteenth and fourteenth centuries), the city was founded on the right bank of the Wad Fez by Idris the Younger in 808, the very year in which he began to exercise power. Although tradition does not furnish any explanation at all on this subject, Idris supposedly founded a second city the following year opposite the first, on the left bank of the river, and established his residence there.

Surprised by this strange fact, the late French scholar E. Lévi-Provençal studied the foundation of Fez closely. He discovered the existence of a tradition less well known but more ancient (tenth century) than the first one. According to this, Idris the Elder founded the city on the right bank of the river before he died, but did not have time to develop it. Some twenty years later, in 809, his son, rather than resume work on a long vegetating building project, founded the city on the left bank. This tradition, supported moreover by the discovery of some coins predating Idris the Younger, appears to be the more probable of the two.

It remains certain at all events that Fez was created by the Idrissides in the first years of the ninth century A.D. at the very latest, and that from then on it consisted of two sections located on both sides of a narrow stream, on the steep slopes of a tight little valley.

The primitive population seems to have been formed of three distinct elements: Arabs attracted by the prestige of the Idrisside family; Berbers of the region; and non-Moslems—Jews and perhaps Christians. Two other groups came soon afterward. These groups consisted of several hundred families driven from Córdoba around 818 and from Kairwan around 825 as an aftermath of popular revolts. Thus, in a short time, Fez received an increment of people accustomed to urban Moslem life. Part of them, at least, were well-informed specialists either in the domain of culture or in that of handicraft techniques. It is probably because of them that Fez took on almost immediately its characteristic aspect of a Moslem city (*madina*). The Andalusians installed themselves in the right-bank city, which took from that time the name of the Andalusian Bank (*'Adwat al-Andalus*); the Kairwanians settled in the left bank city, which became known as the Kairwanian Bank (*'Adwat al-Qarawiyin*).

These promising beginnings led to no immediate developments. Certainly, the two cities grew in population to the point that, as early as the middle of the ninth century, it was necessary to build two important mosques to replace the primitive sanctuaries which had become inadequate. This was the origin of the two celebrated mosques: the Kairwanian (*Jami'al-Qarawiyin*) and the Andalusian (*Jami'al-Andalus*). But the destiny of Fez was linked with that of the Idrisside dynasty. And that dynasty was soon jeopardized by the rivalries of its members and by the attacks of the two great Moslem empires, one in Spain and the other in Ifriqiya (present-day Tunisia), that had come into being at the start of the tenth century. Fez therefore experienced heights and depths during this troubled period that continued until the final third of the eleventh century.

Then, new characters appeared on the Moroccan scene. The Almoravides, Berber camel drivers who came from the western Sahara, were incited chiefly by the religious zeal of new converts to Islam, and also, perhaps, by demographic and economic necessities. They invaded Morocco from the south, founded Marrakech around 1070, extended their conquest toward the north, and occupied Fez no earlier than 1075. Their chief, Yusuf ibn-Tashfin, was a man of great worth and authority. He was aware of the paradox of the twin cities, jealous of each other. He had their separate walls destroyed and replaced by a single rampart which enclosed both of them. He also had the Kairwanian mosque enlarged; it thus became the principal sanctuary of the city. The unification of Fez was an act of primary importance. In addition, the Almoravides made of this city a base of operations for their campaigns in northern Morocco; in central Maghreb, where they conquered Tlemcen and even Algiers; and in Spain, where they were called to defend the Moslems against the Christian Reconquest, and which they soon made a province of their immense empire. If Fez was not the capital of the Almoravides, it was at least one of their principal cities and owed to them, in great part, its rapid development. If one Idris or the other was the original founder of Fez, it can well be said that Yusuf ibn-Tashfin was its second founder, for he unified it and gave it a very important economic and religious impetus.

Fez experienced a fortunate period under the Almoravides and, when their dynasty was threatened, resolutely supported it. But resistance was in vain; for in 1145, after a hard siege, it had to submit to the rule of the conqueror, the Almohade 'Abd al-Mu'min. The Almohades (literally those who proclaim the unity of God) were Berbers from the High Atlas, animated by a zeal for religious reform. They kept Marrakech as their capital. Like the Almoravides, they had to intervene in Spain; like them, they took Fez as the base for their operations and the provisioning of their troops. After a brief eclipse, due to the Almohade war of conquest, Idris's city rapidly resumed its role as a great military and commercial center, and experienced a period of prosperity, attested by the description of the Arab geographer al-Idrisi in the second half of the twelfth century. Under both the Almoravides and the Almohades, Fez received an important increment of Andalusian population in the form of functionaries and specialists of all kinds, employed by the two dynasties. Both dynasties had recourse to the Spanish for the composition of a portion— in all probability the most substantial part—of the administrative staffs of their empires. There is every reason to believe that the high development of technical knowledge in Fez dates from the Almoravide and the Almohade periods, and that under their influence the city took on a more and more marked Andalusian character. It is probable also that under the Almoravide domination Fez received its first Negro inhabitants. The Almoravides themselves were white Berbers, but in the Sahara they were accustomed to using black slaves; and chroniclers report black archers in their army. It may be inferred that they brought Negroes—military or nonmilitary—to Fez, and that some of them settled there and founded families.

In any case, without rising to the first rank, Fez had profited a great deal from the Almoravide and Almohade domination. The two small cities, formerly rivals, had become one important commercial, administrative, and military city. Successively a part of two great empires, it had seen its commerce expand greatly, and its population increase and become enriched by new elements, notably Andalusian scholars who doubtless contributed substantially to its cultural flowering. In short, it may be said that the Almoravides and the Almohades prepared Fez for the role of capital it would be called on to play by the Marinides.

The Marinides entered the history of Morocco around 1215. Up to that time, they formed one Berber tribe among many others, perhaps more or less Arabized, who roved between Figuig and the middle valley of the Moulouya. Sensing the Almohade empire to be less strong than formerly, they ventured into northern Morocco, won some victories over the Almohade troops that were trying to drive them out, and became masters of a large part of the country, with the exception of the cities that remained faithful to the government. It was only in 1248 that the Marinides, profiting by a severe military defeat of the Almohades in the region of Tlemcen, succeeded in seizing Fez and establishing themselves there as sovereigns. However, Almohade power remained in the south of the country, around Marrakech, and a rival Berber dynasty had installed itself at Tlemcen. Finally, in this same year of 1248, the Christians of Castile seized the Moslem city of Seville, after having conquered Valencia and Córdoba a few years before, and gravely threatened the only remaining Moslem territory, the kingdom of Granada and Málaga. The young Marinide state was consequently obliged to wage war rather than think about the improvement of its capital. For a quarter of a century the Almohade city, with an administrative quarter designed for the governor of a province and not for the military and civil services of a state, housed the Marinide court with reasonable adequacy. In all fairness it should be added that, far from remaining constantly in Fez, the Marinide sovereign directed frequent offensive or defensive expeditions toward Marrakech, Tlemcen, and the oasis of Tafilalet, which his rivals were striving to dominate in order to control the terminus of trans-Saharan commerce. At times, he even directed them toward Christian Spain, to assist the Moslems of Granada.

However, the Marinide sovereign Abu Yusuf (1258–86) succeeded in destroying the last Almohades and in conquering Marrakech in 1269; in overawing the ruler of Tlemcen; and in leading victorious expeditions into Spain. His power thus solidly assured, he decided to turn his attention to his capital and to transform it according to his needs. Thus in 1276 he laid the foundations of a new city, Fez Jdid (New Fez), situated in close proximity (about 750 yards) to the already ancient city, where he could, at his convenience, establish his court, his administrative services, and his troops. Consequently, after having been unified by the efforts of Yusuf ibn-Tashfin, Fez resumed its dual aspect through the action of Abu Yusuf the Marinide. But this time it was no longer a question of two rival cities separated only by the width of a river bed. These were two cities of different vocation destined to live side by side. The ancient city (*al-madina*–the city properly termed) was to remain the center of commerce and science and keep its population of old settled citizens. Fez Jdid was elected to become a military and administrative city, inhabited by the sovereign and his family, the dignitaries of the Marinide state, minor officials and servants of all origins, and finally, by the troops recruited in the Marinide tribes or elsewhere.

The military character of Fez Jdid was immediately evident from the strong rampart with which it was invested. On almost its whole circumference this wall was double and reinforced by numerous towers. The city was therefore a stronghold perfectly adapted to its function. It was also the residence of the sovereign and the important men of the state. Several palaces arose there, that of the sovereign eclipsing all the others by its size and richness. Religion was by no means forgotten, for a large and elegant mosque was constructed adjacent to the royal palace when the city was founded. Barracks rounded out the whole. The economic equipment of the new city was restricted to modest proportions, since the markets, warehouses, and workshops of the old city were in full activity and sufficed for the general needs of the two areas. By this construction, Abu Yusuf gave to his dynasty a fitting residence and permitted the two neighboring cities to function comfortably without impeding each other. It was, in short, a very considerable expansion of Fez.

The son and successor of Abu Yusuf, Abu Ya'qub (1286–1307), had an extremely agitated reign, during whose course he had to face several grave revolts and wage an almost continual struggle against the neighboring city of Tlemcen. Consequently he did not have the leisure to pay particular attention to his capital; he limited himself to encouraging the development of Fez Jdid, which had not yet attained its full maturity.

After this bellicose reign, Morocco experienced about twenty-five years of almost total peace. Following the illness and death of two young sultans, power passed into the hands of a brother of Abu Ya'qub, Abu Sa'id 'Uthman, who reigned from 1310 to 1331. He was a peace-loving man who succeeded, on the whole, in avoiding war. Fez profited from peace primarily because it was favorable to commerce and because the court remained in the capital, making its expenditures there. In addition, Fez prospered because Abu Sa'id turned his attention to embellishing the old city, which had scarcely changed since the Almohades.

Abu Yusuf had already built, near the mosque of the Kairwanians, an establishment of learning (*madrasa*) known as the Coppersmiths' *Madrasa* because it was located in the middle of the workshops of the cauldron makers. Abu

Sa'id and his son Abu'l-Hasan had three other *madrasas* built, one at Fez Jdid, near the Great Mosque of this area, which the Marinide sovereign wanted to make a center of education; a second near the Mosque of the Andalusians, forming in reality two *madrasas*, one called the *Madrasa* of the Pool, of vast proportions and beautiful architecture, the other smaller and more specialized, judging by its name: the *Madrasa* of the Seven Fashions of Chanting the Koran. A third *madrasa*, the *Madrasa* of the Perfumers, located near the Mosque of the Kairwanians and the perfume market, was begun in 1323 A.D. and finished two years later. This last *madrasa* was profusely decorated with carved wood, moulded stuccowork, and painted faïence tiling, which make it one of the jewels of Marinide architecture. These embellishments emphasized the interest that the dynasty took in its capital. During the reign of the two following sovereigns, Abu'l-Hasan (1331–51) and Abu 'Inan (1351–58), this solicitude was to manifest itself in a still more evident manner. One after the other, they were to make Fez one of the greatest cities of the Moslem World.

II

FOURTEENTH-CENTURY FEZ

IN THE PERIOD UNDER CONSIDERATION, the city of Fez consisted of two clearly separated sections: the royal city, to be called later on Fez Jdid, known throughout the Marinide period (up to the sixteenth century) under the quasi official name of the White City (*al-madinat al-bayda*); and the ancient city, unified by Yusuf ibn-Tashfin and designated Old Fez (*Fas al-Bali*) or more simply *the* city (*al-madina*). A few suburbs or royal properties situated outside the walls of both cities must be included.

Fez Jdid was first of all a military city: its brownish-red double wall, crowned with merlons and flanked by square towers, pierced by as few gates as possible, well indicates the intention of its founders to make it a stronghold. Built prior to the use of artillery, it was to be reinforced later, at the end of the sixteenth century, by a few bastions capable of supporting cannon. In its fourteenth-century aspect, from whatever side it was approached, it overawed a possible adversary and inspired him with caution. On several of its fronts it was further strengthened by water diverted from the Wad Fez to form a moat at its feet.

The internal aspect of the city did not contradict its external appearance—two quarters were occupied by different corps of the Marinide army. One of them, called by a Moslem chronicler of the period the Christian Suburb, housed the Christian militia, composed of Castilians or

Catalonians whom the Marinides had taken into their service at an early date. Before them, the Almoravides and certain Almohade sovereigns had had Christian soldiers in their service; contemporary with them, the Hafside sovereigns maintained a Catalonian guard in Tunis, setting aside a special quarter for it. Another quarter, situated to the southeast of the White City, served as barracks for the Syrian archers who were at that time part of the Marinide army. It bore the name of Homs, the principal Syrian city of the region where these archers were recruited. About a century later this quarter was to change name and function. In short, the Jews of Fez were cooped up there around 1438. It seems that they had been living in Old Fez from its founding up to that time; then, following incidents that the chroniclers do not report clearly, the Marinide ruler, in order to eliminate existing tension between Moslems and Jews, ordered the latter to settle in a quarter where there were probably no longer any Syrian archers —the Marinide dynasty had suffered severe setbacks and could not now afford luxury troops. With no further reason for existence the name of Homs was replaced little by little in popular usage by that of Mellah, due probably to the fact that a stream rich in salt (*Wad Mellah* means "Salty River") crossed through the quarter or passed nearby.

Apart from military works and barracks, Fez Jdid contained the palace of the sovereign and the residences of the principal dignitaries of the court. It is impossible to say what the palace was like in the period of Abu 'Inan and Abu'l-Hasan, for it underwent so many changes later that even a minute study could only yield uncertain results; such a study has never been made. It is certain that the Marinide palace and its related structures occupied a

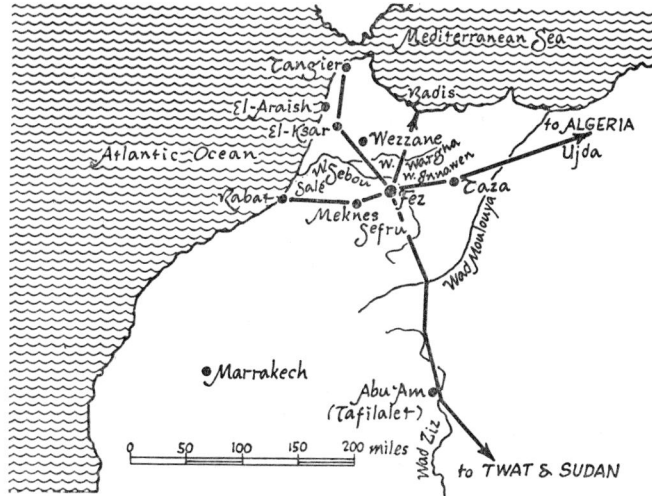

FEZ AS A CROSSROADS IN MOROCCO

much smaller area than the palace of today. As at present, the palace was composed of administrative buildings where the ministers and their aides deliberated, and also of buildings destined to house the ruler, his family, and his servants. Marble, polychrome mosaics, finely moulded stuccowork, ceilings of painted wood, and enormous copper chandeliers upon which oil lamps burned composed the decoration of the palace. The furnishings consisted of mattresses covered with rich materials, thick-pile Berber carpets, and a few pieces of simply carved wooden furniture. The reception rooms opened on courtyards enclosed on all sides; these were floored with little paving stones of painted faïence, interspersed with beds of flowers and fruit trees. In at least some of these courtyards a fountain fell back into a pool gracefully placed in the center. Beside the palace rose the mint, housing at the same time workmen responsible for making silver and gold coins and officials who kept the accounts.

The residences of the court dignitaries were less vast, less richly decorated, but resembled the palace in their general arrangement. They clustered around the palace and the graceful Great Mosque, built by Abu Yusuf. Finally, to the north of the city, a massive gate, flanked on each side by two square crenelated towers, had the majesty requisite for an entrance to a royal city. It was called the Gate of the Lion, probably because of a sculptured motif which has disappeared.

The water supply of this new city was furnished in part by a few wells, but mostly by an aqueduct which brought water from a spring situated a few miles away. Thus, in his wisdom, Sultan Abu Yusuf had chosen to leave all the waters of the Wad Fez at the disposal of the people in the Old City and had avoided grave sources of conflict with this oversensitive and rights-conscious population.

Fez Jdid was a flat city whose boundaries had been laid out by the decree of Abu Yusuf. The Old City was in a quite different situation; it huddled on the slopes—steep in many cases—of a narrow little valley. It had preserved something of its early dual nature. Granted, the two "banks," the Andalusian on the right and the Kairwanian on the left, were enclosed within a single wall. Unquestionably, Yusuf ibn-Tashfin, by enlarging and profusely decorating the Kairwanian Mosque, had manifested his clear intention to give the city a single center, at least in a religious sense. His successors, the Almohades, apparently did not attempt to alter this plan. But so many efforts at unification had not completely eliminated the particularism, perhaps even the hostility, of the two banks. The

action of Abu Sa'id and of his son Abu'l-Hasan, in building *madrasas* near the Andalusian as well as the Kairwanian
Mosque, shows clearly the desire of the Marinides not to
force prematurely a unity which existed physically but not
emotionally.

In fact, Old Fez continued under the Marinides, as it
has remained to the present day, a city with two centers.
To the nucleus on the Kairwanian Bank, formed by the
mosque of the same name and the surrounding bazaar (the
Qisariya, in the language of Fez), corresponded the Andalusian mosque and a more rustic bazaar. The latter drew
less trade and lacked the prestige of the *Qisariya* designa-
tion, but existed nonetheless, and resigned itself only with
reluctance to the superior status of the Kairwanian market.
The dual nature of the *madina* or city must not be exag-
gerated, however. Especially when compared to the new
city of the Marinides, it appears not only as an area enclosed by one single wall, but also as a truly living entity,
proud of its antiquity and its traditions.

The walls still exist; they date from the beginning of
the thirteenth century and have not undergone any important modifications. Like those of Fez Jdid, they are
solid, thick ramparts crowned with pointed merlons and
flanked by square towers. They are pierced by eight gates,
about equally distributed around the circumference of the
enceinte, four on the right bank and the same number on
the left. Certain ones, like the Gate of the Burned Man
(*Bab al-Mahruq*) on the west, were massive; others, whose
description we do not have, were probably only openings
contrived in the wall. All these gates were provided with
strong hinged sections, probably closed every night, and
certainly in case of external threat.

Within the irregular boundary thus defined there were

fairly numerous open spaces near the walls and, from the very first, two vast cemeteries, one for the right bank, to the south of the built-up area, the other for the left bank, to the north. Certainly at that time, as at the beginning of the twentieth century, fairly numerous gardens planted with trees, flowers, and even vegetables, occupied relatively large areas. They were situated, like the cemeteries, along the ramparts, around practically the whole inner circumference of the *enceinte;* at almost no point did the dwellings touch the wall. This was certainly due to breadth of vision on the part of the Almohade builders when marking out the periphery; perhaps it was intended also to allow defenders of the city space to maneuver easily in case of threatened danger. In short, passing the wall did not mean gaining immediate entrance into the city proper, but into a kind of suburb which must have presented a semirural aspect. In that outskirt of the city were established several important industries such as that of the potters, located to the east of the Andalusian Bank, and the olive oil mills, clustered near the gates through which principally olives arrived—Bab Gisa to the north and Bab Ftuh to the south. The sawmills were also grouped around these two gates, which appear to have been the two main economic valves of Fez. Another industrial zone extended along the principal branch of the river, the one which for several centuries had separated the two banks. All the industries which needed water as motive power or as an indispensable work tool were grouped there; primarily the mills, profiting by the rather steep drop of the river toward the interior of the city to make their millstones turn; and the tanneries and dye works, in constant need of water for washing skins or woolen goods. Other industries, with little need for water, had settled there, more or less consciously attracted to an industrial zone created by others. Thus near the river were found the workshops of weavers, shoemakers, makers of brass ware, blacksmiths, and so forth. In short, three principal industrial zones could be distinguished: that of the north, around Bab Gisa; that of the south, around Bab Ftuh; that of the center, on both sides of the river. Naturally this does not mean that there were no industrial establishments elsewhere: weavers, shoemakers and cobblers, blacksmiths, jewelers and many others were scattered through almost all the quarters of the city.

As in the case of industry, commerce was in a large measure concentrated in one area. Near the principal gates (Bab Gisa, Bab Ftuh, Bab al-Mahruq) were located several wholesale markets, notably those of grains: this avoided transporting heavy, cumbersome merchandise in large quantities through the narrow streets. In the center of the city, near the Kairwanian Mosque, spread out the *Qisariya*, which could be compared to a large modern store. There customers found most of the objects they needed: cloth, jewels, perfumes and spices, leather goods, books, candles and lamps, and footwear. The neighboring bazaar of the Andalusian Mosque duplicated this one, but on a smaller scale. The *Qisariya* was not composed solely of shops; quite near the latter rose the warehouses named *funduq*, where wholesalers stocked merchandise imported from outside the city, before selling it to the retailers of the *Qisariya*. There was scarcely any need to stock the products of local industry; their makers took them to a public auction held generally near the *Qisariya*, in the courtyard of a *funduq*, or else in the lanes of the *Qisariya* itself. The storekeepers bought them there and placed them in their small shops. Foodstuffs and products for daily use, such as household utensils and dishes, were offered to the public in neighborhood markets. These were to be found along all the most important thoroughfares, that is to say, distributed throughout the built-up areas.

The zones that would now be called residential were located in between the different industrial and commercial quarters. The residences communicated with the street only by an offset entrance, and several dormer windows which permitted the identification of visitors before they were allowed to enter. The dwellings received air and light from their interior court, for they were all built around a patio, more or less large, where there was no risk of the women's being seen from the outside. As these patios were sometimes small in size, the women had another more airy domain which was theirs alone: the terraces, for all the houses of Fez had these flat roofs. Toward the center of the city the houses stood close together and the patios were small; toward the outer edge they were farther apart and the patios were of larger size.

Public buildings, aside from the mosques, were not very numerous. In fact, the administrative buildings were located in Fez Jdid, with the exception of the offices of the governor of the old city, which had remained in the fortress built at its western end by the Almohades. There was no equivalent of the city hall or of the town hall common to European cities of the Middle Ages, since, as will be seen, the municipal administration was entirely in the hands of the central power, and of diminished importance. The existence of a hospital in the neighborhood of the *Qisariya* should be mentioned; it was restored by Abu'l-Hasan and was, in actual fact, destined for the care of the insane. This building, like all the *madrasas* and the mosques, had a clearly religious character. Therefore it can be asserted that almost all the public buildings of Fez had, in principle, a religious objective.

The *madrasas* were student lodgings more than schools, properly speaking. To those built by the first Marinides, Abu'l-Hasan and his son Abu 'Inan were each to add one. The first was built in 1346 or 1347, by Abu'l-Hasan, quite near the Kairwanian Mosque and the *Madrasa* of the Perfumers. It is known today under the name of the Misbah *Madrasa*, probably in honor of a famous professor who taught there. However, it has often been called the Marble *Madrasa* because it was decorated with a beautiful fountain of marble imported by Abu'l-Hasan from Almería in Spain, and brought to Fez by way of the Sebou River—one of the rare occasions when this stream served as a navigable waterway. After 1351, at an unspecified date, Abu 'Inan built the largest and most sumptuous of the *madrasas* of Fez, which still bears his name (the Abu 'Inan *Madrasa*); it is located in the higher, western part of the old city. In this *madrasa* and in it alone were built large rooms which could only be lecture halls. It was thus intended from the beginning to be not only a student lodging, but also an autonomous establishment of learning. All these *madrasas* were provided with a hall for prayers, a hall for ablutions, and a pool, or a fountain basin in the middle of the courtyard, for minor ablutions. Two of them, the Coppersmiths' *Madrasa* and the Abu 'Inan *Madrasa* also included a minaret. The second was even provided with a pulpit, which proves that the solemn Friday prayer was celebrated there. These were consequently private chapels for the students, and, in addition, places of prayer for the faithful of the neighborhood. Student lodgings, parish churches, and works of art as well—such were the *madrasas* of Fez, almost all of Marinide origin. Only one other, in fact, was built, around 1670, by the first ruler of the 'Alawite dynasty, Mulay al-Rashid, in the immediate vicinity of the Kairwanian Mosque.

As for the mosques, they were primarily places of prayer, but they served also as meeting places for public and private business. It was in the mosques, on the occasion of the solemn Friday prayer, that official government proclamations were read. The Friday sermon began by an invocation to God in behalf of the Prophet and his immediate successors, and also the reigning sovereign. When power was disputed among several rivals, the Friday sermon took on great political importance. Fathers who were going to arrange the marriage of a son and daughter also met in the mosques: after the recitation of the first sura of the Koran, they received the congratulations of their friends who had come to attend the ceremony. The betrothals were thus celebrated in the presence of God. Many business affairs were also concluded in the mosques, so that the conditions agreed upon might in this way assume a ceremonial, spiritual character. Lastly, before a body was carried to the cemetery, a stop was made at the mosque of the district to ask God for eternal repose for the deceased. The body was placed not in the prayer hall, for a corpse carries with it defilement, but in a special room adjoining the prayer hall, called the funeral hall. Thus the place held by the mosque in the life of the citizens of Fez is easy to see; it is not surprising that these were imposing and elaborate buildings whose sentimental prestige and emotional influence were no less great than their architectural design.

The Marinides constructed few mosques in the old city of Fez, already well endowed with them before their time.

The 'Alawite sovereigns were to build even more there from the seventeenth to the nineteenth centuries. It is true that the Marinides had to build several mosques in Fez Jdid. In addition to the Great Mosque, built when the city was founded, they raised another on the main street, probably at the beginning of the fourteenth century, known as the Red Mosque. Two others, Lalla Ghriba and the Mosque of the Flower, were built in the fifteenth century in the Fez Jdid area. In the old city only two important mosques are their work: The Mosque of the Bootmakers and that of Abu'l-Hasan, both located on the Kairwanian Bank, proof that in their time this part of the city felt new needs, while the Andalusian Bank scarcely underwent any change.

Traffic within the city of Fez was naturally taken care of by streets. However, they resembled neither the wide, straight streets of Roman cities, nor even the winding but relatively broad streets of European cities of the Middle Ages. The reason for this was that the use of wheeled vehicles was unknown in Fez, as in almost all cities of North Africa. The inhabitants circulated on foot or, in the case of wealthier persons, on magnificent mules, well fed and groomed to sleekness. Merchandise was transported on the backs of men or of beasts of burden: donkeys, mules, or horses. Therefore there was no need at all for wide arteries of traffic: space for two loaded animals to pass was sufficient. Besides, urban planning did not exist in North Africa in the Middle Ages; the street system of Old Fez apparently developed according to random circumstance and prior occupation of the land by private property owners. Consequently the streets, even the important ones, often zigzagged, skirting private property. There existed, however, large arteries that connected as directly as possible the two centers of the Kairwanian and Andalusian banks with each other, by means of three bridges over the river, and with the three principal gates of the city: those of the north, south, and west, through which passed the main external traffic of Fez. It should be mentioned, however, that these streets were blocked by gates and closed at night or in case of disturbance. Each quarter could, in the latter case, try to isolate itself from the rest of the city; access was regularly shut off each evening after nightfall. Consequently, it was difficult to circulate during the night, first because there was no public lighting and each person had to provide himself with a lantern, and also because it was necessary to have the gates opened in case of passage from one quarter to another. The latter necessitated either awakening the guards who were sometimes asleep, or else waiting for their return if they were making their rounds at the other end of the quarter. Outside the main arteries, the number of blind alleys was great. In fact, Moslem cities of North Africa were not laid out according to street plans; the location of the streets was determined by the arrangement of the buildings. As a result, there were numerous dead-end passages winding between houses in order to provide access to those located in the center of a residential block.

On the other hand, the system of water distribution was quite remarkable. The slope of the terrain and the existence of numerous springs within the city facilitated it, of course, but the skill of the engineers made admirable use of these propitious conditions. It is probable that the system still in use at the present time dates from the Almoravide or the Almohade period. The engineers of that time distributed the waters of the Wad Fez, upstream from the city, into several artificial channels which permitted bringing the water into almost all quarters and even into almost all residences of the old city. Only the quarters situated in the southeastern part were somewhat at a disadvantage from this point of view, but they supplemented their supply from numerous wells. It can therefore be said that in the Marinide period almost all the old city of Fez had running water and, naturally, a parallel system of drains, which, thanks to the slope, permitted easy return of waste waters into the river. Few medieval cities were as well provided for as Fez in this respect. This abundance of water permitted the building of numerous public fountains where animals and people could drink without cost. In addition, all the mosques had the pool and water hall indispensable to ritualistic ablutions. And finally, the city possessed numerous establishments of public baths; some were built in the Marinide period but the majority existed well before that time.

The population of the old city was quite different from that of Fez Jdid. While the latter was almost entirely made up of soldiers, dignitaries, and civil servants of the Marinide regime, people not long accustomed to urban life, the inhabitants of the old city were for the most part city dwellers of long standing. It is most probable that the Berber element, dominant in the beginning, was now scarcely distinguishable from the others. In any case, it is certain that in the fourteenth century Arabic was the sole language currently spoken in Fez: even the few latecomers whose maternal language was Berber were capable of understanding Arabic and of expressing themselves in that language.

The predominant element in the city was the middle class of Arabic, Berber, Andalusian, or Kairwanian origin; a few traces of a kind of pride of caste or of particularist feeling possibly persisted in an occasional family. But almost all had become, in fact, "people of Fez" (*ahl Fas*, as is still said in Arabic)—that is to say, citizens of the town, entitled to live there because they had long since adopted its usages and customs, its decorum (*al-qa'ida*). Thus they were conscious of participating in a refined and essentially superior life. These middle class people could not refrain from showing condescension with regard to the rustics of the surrounding countryside. They surpassed them often, if not always, in material wealth and in good manners, but they were especially conscious of superiority in self-possession, social ease, intellectual alertness, and, most important, in piety. While the country people knew poorly or only moderately well the law and even the ritual of Islam, while their piety remained stuck fast in censurable superstitions, the people of Fez had the good conscience of the Pharisees of the Scriptures. It should be added objectively that they were not always wrong, but that neither were they as right as they thought.

This middle class was composed of three categories of persons. First were the merchants, in the sense of wholesalers or dealers in luxury merchandise whose business was primarily local but extended sometimes over the whole of Morocco (certain products of Fez were sold as far as Marrakech and beyond); into the black country of Africa, thanks to the caravans; into Europe through the medium of several Mediterranean ports where Venetian, Genoese, and Provençal vessels called regularly; and lastly, into the rest of North Africa and even into Egypt, thanks to the Pilgrimage, which was at the same time a business trip and the accomplishment of a religious obligation. The profits realized were invested in business on the one hand, but served also for the acquisition of real property: urban real estate, gardens within the *enceinte* or in its immediate vicinity, agricultural properties, within a radius of about 30 miles around the city. Beside these businessmen, and, for the most part, closely involved with them by family relationships, lived the men of learning—professors at the Moslem University, or intellectuals without official function, who enjoyed great esteem and often also great material affluence. Among them figured some students from the country, who, thanks to their work and their intellectual aptitudes, had succeeded in making a place for themselves among the intelligentsia of Fez. But, as a general rule, the majority of intellectuals belonged to families long established in the city. Lastly, others—often of more or less remote Andalusian origin, but of Berber origin too—served as functionaries in the government and staffed the state bureaus. Their station appears to have been completely analogous to that of the two preceding categories.

Below this élite, and often linked with it by family ties, by personal relationships, but especially by the fact of participating in the same urban civilization, came the mass of small merchants and artisans. The latter had far less means than the others, for minor commerce and industry provided a comfortable living but not a fortune. They were chiefly of Berber origin, but had long since left their mountain or plains tribe and had become little by little bona fide citizens, in the ethical sense of the word. They had adopted the clothing, the manners and customs, the civilization of Fez, and through matrimonial alliances, good luck, and cleverness had a chance to become someday part of the élite.

Below them lived the group, numerous in all probability, of newcomers to the city, men or women of tribes coming to Fez to seek their fortune, or to escape famine, or else to flee from family or tribal vengeance. In general, they began very humbly as unskilled workers or day laborers: this was especially the case of those who cultivated the gardens of the property owners of Fez. They lived in the external quarters of the city, those nearest the gates through which they had entered: quarters which still preserved a rustic aspect, where poultry and cows were raised, where residences were neither tall nor luxurious. Some did not succeed in adapting to city life and returned sooner or later to the original tribe, on the occasion of a marriage or a favorable agricultural year. Others, on the contrary, settled down in Fez, learned a trade, and ended by increasing the number of artisans and shopkeepers, with the hope of one day becoming part of the élite of the city. Among these neo-city dwellers particular mention should be made of seasonal workers. For example, immediately after the olive harvest, the oil mills of Fez worked at full speed and needed additional laborers. Certain tribes, especially from the regions north of Fez, profiting from the fact that agricultural work slackened at that time, sent part of their workmen to Fez for the few weeks during which they were needed. A group of these temporary workers was composed of Berbers from the Upper Guir region, some two hundred miles to the southeast of Fez, who came to offer their services as porters. According to tradition, these Berbers had been coming to work in Fez since the founding of the city, in the time of Mawlay Idris. These were all young and vigorous men who spent in Fez the few months or years needed for saving the money which would permit a return to their tribe for marriage and the acquiring of a little property.

Finally the old city of Fez housed a Jewish community whose size is impossible to estimate, but which appears to have been substantial. It was probably a question, at least in a large majority of cases, of Berbers converted to Judaism at a remote period and still preserving the faith of their fathers. It is impossible to assert that they lived in a special quarter, but this is probable if one takes into account the toponymy of Fez, where a whole quarter is still known by the name of *Funduq al-Ihudi* (The Warehouse of the Jew), in the neighborhood of Bab Gisa, the northern gate of the city. Certain of these Jews engaged in commerce on a large scale and had reached an enviable financial situation; others devoted themselves to study and assumed religious functions or participated in administration of the community which, in all matters of personal regulation, lived according to the Hebraic law. The majority, according to all probability, were shopkeepers or artisans; several trades, like the working of precious metals, were reserved for them in practice if not by law. It seems that all these Jews were concentrated on the Kairwanian Bank and that there were none either in Fez Jdid, where they were to establish themselves in the following century, or on the Andalusian Bank.

At last, under the Marinides, Fez had put forth a few feelers, extending even beyond the walls. The city was able to come out of its shell, proof of the great sense of security that the Marinides had succeeded in creating in all the surrounding countryside. This was contrary to its later history when, from the early seventeenth century on, Fez, like most other Moroccan cities, timidly drew back inside its walls.

The great weekly market, to be called later on the Thursday Market (*Suq al-Khamis*), was first held outside the walls in the vicinity of the west gate. Whether this market was already held only on Thursday or whether in reality it took place twice a week, as was the case later on, is impossible to verify. It is certain that this market existed and that it had great importance. In fact, it constituted the normal meeting ground of city and country dwellers. The latter came to sell their animals: oxen and calves, sheep, goats, mules, donkeys, horses, turkeys, chickens; and, in addition, products of their humble industry, such as pieces of earthenware or some lengths of cloth, woven and decorated with simple designs. The country people met there not only customers but also a few merchants of Fez who offered them slippers, cloth, and implements for husbandry without their needing to enter a city which was strange to them and where lack of familiarity meant a risk of getting lost. They also found a blacksmith to repair their tools, farriers to shoe their animals, vendors of amulets and remedies, and finally, storytellers and mountebanks to amuse them. On fine days—and these predominate in Fez— it was a sort of weekly fair to which country dwellers came from twelve to twenty miles around, from which they brought back a little money, if they were able to resist the thousand temptations of a big city, and where they received news and exchanged opinions. Thus the Thursday Market was not only an economic event, but also an occasion for recreation and a means for fostering and moulding rural public opinion.

To the north of Fez Jdid, on the gentle slope of a hill crowned with olive trees, one of the Marinide sovereigns, probably Abu Yusuf, had a royal garden laid out; it contained two pools, vestiges of which can still be seen. These pools, serving at least as much for irrigation of the garden as for pleasure of the sovereign and his guests, were fed by action of an immense wooden wheel, situated near the Gate of the Lion. This wheel raised water from the river to the height of an aqueduct which carried it to the pools. This must have been a charming spot when the trees planted there had attained their normal growth and the flowers were in bloom. It stood slightly above the royal city; from it could be seen the high quarters of the old city, the vast and beautiful panorama of the Saïs Plain, and the often snow-covered mountains of the Middle Atlas. Buildings had been erected in this beautiful garden and distinguished guests were lodged in them.

In a period impossible to fix precisely, but which must not have been far removed from the one under consideration, a Marinide ruler had had a country home (*manzah*) built on the hill which immediately overlooks the old city of Fez on the north. This hill received later on the name of Marinide Tombs, because a cemetery climbed up it little by little; but in the beginning there was only a country home, with a little private chapel whose remains can still be seen. The old city of Fez spread out below in all its expanse; farther on, hills of olive trees billowed up toward the summits of the Middle Atlas. This was a magnificent landscape; a sovereign's wish to enjoy it from a pleasant residence is understandable. In addition, there is mention in the chronicles of a leprosarium, situated in a solitary valley to the northwest of the old city. Lastly, to the west of the old city and to the north of Fez Jdid, several sections composed of ramshackle buildings, probably resembling the shantytowns of our time except in construction materials, housed families of workers newly arrived from the country. They preferred this still largely rural area to the crowded city dwellings where they would have felt hemmed in. There was even a village of washermen to the west of Fez Jdid, on the banks of the river. There were probably also in these external suburbs, if the chroniclers are trustworthy, vagrants who preferred to live where they could easily escape the surveillance of the police.

The general impression, therefore, is of a lively and fairly stable city, provided with all the diverse conveniences that comfort-loving citizens of that period could wish for.

III

CITY ADMINISTRATION

IT MUST FIRST BE MADE CLEAR that in the Marinide period the reference is not to one city but to two, without counting the suburbs installed outside the ramparts. Fez Jdid and the old city were, in reality, two entirely distinct administrative units. No information is available as to the manner in which the built-up areas *extra muros* were administered, if they were at all. With the exception of the leprosarium, which was certainly under the administration of religious properties, these areas give the impression of temporary groupings, originating outside urban institutions and their restraints, that did not seek to incorporate themselves into an established framework.

No precise information concerning the administration of Fez Jdid exists, but from the little that is known, three elements, each different from the other, can be pointed out. In the first place, the palace and its dependent structures were evidently subject to the direct authority of the sovereign and the high officials who surrounded him; these included ministers, but were chiefly officers of the royal household who tyrannized over the lesser tribe of functionaries, and of servingmen and serving-women. In the second place, the military units who lived in this garrison city were placed under the authority of their direct superiors and the commanders of the army. Lastly, the civil population of Fez Jdid, composed largely of dignitaries and agents of the state, probably had its own institutions: a governor, a military man perhaps, but who was directly under the authority of the sovereign, and a cadi, possibly the cadi of the army. There never seems to have been in Fez Jdid the provost of the guilds found in the old city; economic life was too elementary there to require such a functionary. Neither is there found any trace of the quarter system which existed in the neighboring city. Its districts were the palace, the barracks, and the residential zone of the officials: each of these organizations had its own institutions which resembled only faintly an arrangement by quarters. It can be said, in short, that Fez Jdid was a city placed too directly in the shadow of the royal power and too deeply diversified to foster the development of true urban institutions.

The situation was quite different in the old city. The few hundred yards which separated it from the royal city made it a completely different world, from the administrative point of view.

It was governed by three functionaries, all named by the sovereign or his ministers: the governor, the cadi, and the *muhtasib* or provost of the guilds. The governor was the direct representative of the sovereign and was wholly devoted to him, for his career depended upon him. He saw that his master's decisions were carried out, was responsible for the maintenance of order, and was in this capacity chief of police; and he judged affairs of penal or criminal character. Also, he was responsible for the execution of the sentences he pronounced: imprisonment and sometimes public bastinado. He was, if such an expression may be hazarded in a Moslem country, a purely secular functionary: religion had nothing to do with his appointment or with the greater part of his activities. He resided in the fortress built or rebuilt by the Almohades to the west of the city. Was he a military man? The question is somewhat idle in connection with a state where the distinction now made between military and civil status was practically nonexistent, where there were no army or civil administration careers, but only careers in the service of the prince.

The cadi, on the other hand, was an essentially religious official. His primary function consisted of promoting the reign of justice in conformity with the law—thus he carried out not the orders of the sovereign but the decrees of God himself. He was, therefore, first of all, a magistrate who settled all disputes over personal status, relying upon the text of the Koran, and all the jurisprudence which had little by little accrued to this text. As a result, the cadi was necessarily an educated man who must have a profound knowledge of juridical theory and practice. He could not then be solely (as was the governor) a career man whose personal qualities of cleverness, decision, and versatility were his cardinal points; he was first of all a cultivated man, almost a scholar. It is needless to insist on the moral authority that the cadi could wield through his judiciary functions: if he combined a thorough knowledge of the law and a good portion of fairness, he could make harmony reign in the city; if he did not, he appeared as a factor of disorder and demoralization. It is a heavy task to be the sole judge in a city inhabited by nearly 100,000 persons, according to all probability; consequently the cadi was assisted by a deputy—a specialist, it appears, in matters of marriage and divorce. However, the cadi was not solely a judge: his office conferred upon him also the control of all the pious foundations, which seem to have been considerable in number from the Marinide period on. Granted, the pious foundations were purely religious in purpose. But it is well known that in Islam, Cæsar's domain and God's are closely identified, as Cæsar is supposed to be on earth only a faithful servant of God. Consequently, pious foundations did not serve exclusively for the maintenance of religious worship and the buildings pertaining to it, nor yet the proper progress of education, but also for the functioning of what would be called, in modern terms, public services, such as those of hospitals, the majority of the public baths, etc. . . . In short, the pious foundations furnished a good share of the city revenues, and the cadi was the controller of the municipal budget. In this capacity, he had under his orders a whole administration of tax-gatherers, controllers, and accountants who managed considerable funds. And lastly, in his role of principal representative of the law, the cadi traditionally controlled orthodoxy—intellectual life and instruction. He might almost be called the rector of the Kairwanian University. Sole judge, person responsible for a large part of the city's finances, rector of the University, and censor of intellectual life—the importance of the cadi's role is easy to see. He might have been tempted to take advantage of it if he had not been a man of learning and a respectful servant of the law, and if, in addition, like all the other functionaries, he had not been subject to the absolute authority of the sovereign. There is no example under the Marinides of a cadi's having tried to use his influence to play a larger role.

The third functionary, the *muhtasib*, was a curious personage resembling at the same time the censor of the Roman Republic and the Greek *agoranomos*. Like the cadi, he was in the service of the religious law, but on a more practical level, since he was charged with overseeing the application of Moslem ethics in the daily life of the city. He was, therefore, a sort of prefect of manners, and in this capacity he had the surveillance of the public baths and also of the prostitutes, but his principal role consisted of safeguarding the honesty of the exchanges, and by this fact he controlled economic life in large measure. He directed the inspection of weights and measures and had had sealed into the wall of the *Qisariya* a standard cubit which permitted verification of good measure received. It is certain that he had standard weights established as well, but they have not been found. He watched also the quality of the products sold, whether foodstuffs or articles made by the artisans of Fez. Anyone who was caught cheating was liable to punishment; details will be given farther on. Finally, in case of legal disputes in the artisans' corporations, and perhaps in the merchants' corporations (but this last point is not clearly ascertainable), he served as arbitrator. He intervened thus in quarrels between employers and workmen, or else between two proprietors, or even a seller and his customer. In order to settle these differences, he had the assistance of experts chosen from among the best representatives of the corporation, according to a method which will be examined later. That the *muhtasib* was obliged to have a good knowledge of the Moslem law goes without saying; but he had also to be well versed in the usages of Fez, almost as important as the law, which did not treat technical questions in detail. He was then necessarily a man born into a family long established in the city, a man whose integrity was unquestioned. He had at his disposition a few executive assistants, but these were limited in number; the responsibility of his office really rested upon him.

These three functionaries and their collaborators constituted the administration of the city. In principle, they were subordinate only to the sovereign or his ministers and had no account to render to anyone else. In actual fact, this was not quite true, for if the administrative organization of Moslem countries in the Middle Ages was founded primarily on the principle of authority, it had to take into account another fundamental principle of Moslem public equity: the duty of responsible leaders to get complete information on an affair before arriving at a decision. This duty of consultation, *mushawara* in Arabic, has never been codified under the form of permanent statutes, but it has been none the less a matter of practice. Likewise the sovereign, for serious affairs of state, generally made inquiries of the scholars, to ascertain that his decisions were not contrary to the law, and of the notables, to measure carefully the reactions of public opinion. In the same way the cadi, and even more frequently the governor and the *muhtasib*, had both the opportunity and the duty to consult people competent in the matters which were under their jurisdiction. It has just been mentioned that the *muhtasib* surrounded himself with councils of experts in order to settle the disputes submitted to him. It may certainly be assumed also that he did not fix the market price of the principal articles of trade without recourse to competent advice. The cadi himself, when censoring the intellectual life of the city, had recourse to the counsel of the principal scholars of the Mosque of the Kairwanians. Finally, the governor was in contact with the population through the intermediary of the chiefs of the quarters.

The old city of Fez was in fact divided into a certain number of quarters. The details of this division during the Marinide period are not known precisely. It may be inferred, however, that it was probably not very different from that existing in the nineteenth century: at that time the old city was divided into eighteen quarters, twelve on the Kairwanian Bank, six on the Andalusian. Moreover, the important fact is that the quarters existed, whatever may have been their number and boundaries in the Marinide period. Each had at its head a chief named by the governor, but on recommendation of the influential men of the quarter. This district chief was therefore at the same time the representative of the central administration, since he was appointed by it, but also of those under his jurisdiction, since his name had been proposed by them. In actuality, he was not the elected representative of the people of his district in the modern sense of the expression: he was not put into office by a majority vote. His name was proposed by the notables of the quarter, who came to an agreement among themselves for its presentation and arrived generally at unanimity. In fact Moslem practice is averse, practically even in our time, to making use of the brutal law of the majority. It finds preferable discussions during whose course opinions begin by clashing but, after long contact with each other, finish by losing their sharp disjunction, and end in a compromise generally acceptable to all. The district chief thus named had a delicate position, because he was at the same time the man of the government that appointed him and of the influential men of the quarter who recommended him. This double relationship gave him the role of an intermediary quite in conformity to procedures in Moslem public life. He spent a portion of his time getting in contact with governmental services in order to understand their point of view well, and to inform them of the reactions of the notables of his quarter. Then he apprized the latter of the authorities' intentions and took note of their views, not without trying to make them concur with the official intent. In the majority of cases he succeeded in this compromise, which seems to be the essential aim of politics, at least in Islamic countries. Unfortunately, no precise information is available on the district chiefs of Fez in the Marinide period. It is not certain that they were themselves a part of the group of notables whose characterization will be presently attempted. If, as is probable, political customs in Fez have not changed much through the centuries, it can almost be asserted that the district chiefs were not numbered among the influential men much in the public eye. In the difficult role played by them, outstanding notables would too often have risked finding themselves in uncomfortable situations where their prestige, sometimes even their wealth, would have been in danger. They therefore preferred to leave this post to men with less to lose. This does not mean that district chiefs were men of low birth; their work required, on the contrary, marked qualities of composure, skill, experience, and sometimes courage. But these were men without a long past history in the city; by exercising their function and making a success of it they gained the opportunity to assume their place among the principal influential men.

The concept of a notable was not a legally imposed idea, but a concept of practical fact, as changeable and vague as life itself. The heads of old and esteemed families were among the influential of a quarter; rich families had their place there too; but learning—knowledge of the Moslem law and Arabo-Islamic culture—counted for a great deal. Also included among the influential were those who expressed themselves easily in an assembly and knew how to present and impose their opinion. Finally, pious persons, those who were tinged with a reasonable mysticism, also had their word to say. It may be seen from this enumeration that the notables of a quarter could be numerous and came from varied backgrounds. They represented at the same time economic interests, intellectual and religious values, prestige of tradition, and personal qualities independent of all these. Although detailed information about daily life in the quarters during the fourteenth century is not available, it may be inferred without too much risk of error that in each district five or six persons, influential for different reasons, were the moulders of opinion, and that it was with these men especially that the district chief had to reckon. The important thing, in any case, is this influence of opinion exercised in actual fact upon those bearing the responsibility for municipal administration. When it was a question of important affairs, transcending the quarter boundaries and of concern to the whole city, contact was established directly between the governor and the notables of the city: then the governor found himself face to face with the important men of each quarter who met to discuss with him the matters involved. It must be clearly understood that none of this was of a statutory character: assemblies of notables from the entire city had no official entity; there were no meetings on fixed dates, no dignitaries regularly designated. It may be assumed that, according to the occasion, the decisive influence belonged now to men of learning, now to representatives of economic interests, and again to the heads of the oldest families. Essentially pragmatic in character, this is very different from the democratic institutions of our time. It resulted, nonetheless, in a sort of permanent control over the wielders of authority, exercised by the most representative men of the city.

The holders of authority were assisted in their daily tasks by what would now be called public services. It must be made clear that these public services, like our own, were at the disposition of the public, but that they were not always—even not often—collectively organized, as are ours in many cases. They were often private enterprises, controlled in general by the authorities and put at the disposal of the public.

In a city like Fez, the most important public services were probably those concerned with water. It has been seen earlier that the old city possessed, for the conveyance and evacuation of water, a system quite exceptional for the period. This system naturally required constant maintenance without which it could easily become unusable. Of primary importance was the task of keeping in good operating condition the open canals which, leading directly from the river, channeled water toward the different quarters. These canals had to be cleaned out periodically, especially after times of heavy rain when the river swept along quantities of mineral, vegetable, and even animal debris; in addition, the violence of the current sometimes caused caving in of the banks, which had to be remedied. Each quarter had the right to a certain quantity of water, measured by means of a distributor. These distributors had to be verified regularly so that no one would fail to receive his due. Once the water was started toward the quarters and private properties, it passed through underground conduits made by the potters of Fez, where water circulated by simple gravity, as the general slope of the terrain permitted. As for waste waters, they were evacuated by the same procedure as far as the river, downstream from the city or as near as possible to the spot where it emerged from the city.

When or how the first distribution of the new waters was made is unknown. It may be supposed that this dated at least from the unification and development of Fez in the Almoravide epoch, and probably had even more ancient origins; it was certainly minutely detailed and must have provoked numerous disputes. No information prior to the eighteenth century is available concerning the maintenance of the water distribution system in Fez, but there is every reason to think that the organization in force at that time was much more ancient and had already been functioning for a long period in the Marinide epoch. It included two sorts of technicians: specialized workers capable of detecting and repairing rapidly any unexpected breaks, and experts in water rights, thoroughly grounded in the customs of Fez and the variations inevitably produced by purchases, sales, and, especially, the contingent division of properties.

The experts in water rights, often well-known jurists, had other occupations and devoted only a part of their time to these questions; on the other hand, the canal technicians constituted a permanent group. It is probable, although no precise information on this point can be had, that they received a fixed salary from the service of religious properties, and that in case of repairs they received a special remuneration probably supplied by the users, whether these were private parties or the pious foundations which maintained the numerous public fountains and hydraulic installations of the mosques and public baths.

However extensive the system of water distribution, it did not cover all needs. Certain sections were at too high an elevation to be reached by the canals. There were therefore in Fez, as in most cities of the Middle Ages, water carriers who furnished the unsupplied houses, and circulated in public places to permit passers-by to quench their thirst. They frequented notably the markets, the pilgrimage shrines, and the places where storytellers and mountebanks plied their trades. They carried slung over the shoulder a large bottle made of goat skin, carefully stitched and on which the hair had been left; to their belts were attached copper goblets into which they poured water for their customers. Their apparatus was completed by a little bell, rung often to make their presence known. If it was a question of supplying a dwelling with water, they filled little wooden casks and transported them on donkeyback to where they were needed. Their recompense came solely from their customers and the *muhtasib* watched only over their honesty and, it is to be hoped, over their cleanliness. They took part also in fire fighting, for there never seems to have existed in Fez the equivalent of our modern firemen. When a fire broke out, the water carriers rushed up with their filled goat skins and casks, assisted by all those who possessed a container of sufficient size, notably the tanners and the dyers, whose occupation obliged them to have buckets permanently at hand. Of course, all men in the vicinity of the disaster also lent a helping hand, on the principle of reciprocity. In this city where wood formed a large part of the construction of homes, where cooking was done in the open air on little charcoal stoves, where, in addition, summer heat and drying winds were not rare, fires were much to be feared, and sometimes spread widely, especially in the markets and warehouses where the stored goods could feed them. That is why night watchmen slept in the markets: they were charged with preventing fires, and also thefts, to the fullest extent possible.

Water constituted the essential raw material of the public baths. These baths *(Hamman)* were located in all the quarters of the city, and there were even several in the densely populated quarters, without counting the private baths installed in opulent residences. Almost all the public baths had been constructed by the service of religious properties. They were rented to contractors who managed them in exchange for a fixed sum, paid to the service of religious properties. The clients were of two kinds. First were the individuals who came to take a bath for a price publicly posted, and which varied according to the establishment, for there were more or less luxurious ones, and ones more or less well known. The baths were open to men all morning and to women all afternoon, with an interval of two or three hours between the two sessions for cleaning and filling the boiler. When women were at the bath a cord was stretched across the door; it was the sign that men were not supposed to enter. The second kind of client was the family who rented the bath for one night, most of the time for the organization of certain ritual ceremonies such as the bath of the bride or of the newly delivered mother. In this case, the rental price varied according to the number of participants and the importance of the ceremony. In any case, the bath was not solely a place for getting clean: it had a great religious importance since it permitted the accomplishment of ritual purifications, and a social importance, since several essential family ceremonies took place there. It was therefore indispensable for these establishments to be closely supervised so that they were always in good operating condition, and also so that morality prevailed there. That is why the *muhtasib* had control over them. The bathing establishment was analogous to the thermal baths of antiquity. It included a room for undressing, a cold room, a tepid room, and a hot room, and lastly a quiet room for resting where the clients, dressed once more, relaxed after the fatigues of the bath, or else had themselves massaged by men or women specializing in this work, or even had themselves shaved by barbers. All these rooms were dimly lighted so that modesty might be preserved.

Also connected with water usage was the maintenance of refuse disposal service. It consisted first of all in the removal of household wastes. Until the nineteenth century, when European travelers vied with each other in indignation over the filthy condition of the streets of Fez, there is no mention of the humble but indispensable task of refuse removal in a large city. Questions may be asked but they cannot be answered. It is not known whether there was a service of refuse removal and how it functioned, or whether individuals were obliged to make provision themselves for the removal of their waste materials. In that case, those who lived near the river were in the most favored situation: all they had to do was to throw refuse into the water. As for the others, they carried it or had it carried to a rubbish heap outside the nearest city gate.

But, outside of household wastes, the street could be soiled by the droppings of animals (there were a great many of them circulating in the streets of Fez), by dust, and by mud. It is not known whether streets were cleaned in the Marinide period in the same way that travelers saw it done in the nineteenth century: from time to time, on the order of the governor, a canal was opened onto one of the principal streets and a veritable torrent rushed down the steep incline to the river, carrying everything with it as it passed by—the filth perhaps, but also all the objects which might be along the edge of the street.

Naturally there was a police force placed under the orders of the governor of the city and the chiefs of the quarters. Leo Africanus affirms that there were in Fez only four police commissioners who made rounds in the middle of the night; it may be inferred that they were assisted by deputies, but that these were few in number.

It is quite probable that, as was the case several centuries later, criminality was rare in Fez—not that people were more virtuous there than elsewhere, but because, in that city of stable population, where life in the local quarter was well developed, where everybody was acquainted, and all were informed about the habits of each individual, it was materially difficult to get off the beaten track. The role of the police consisted therefore in preserving order and peace, in settling little neighborhood quarrels, and above all, in keeping under surveillance the gates and ramparts, in order to prevent suspicious and unknown characters from penetrating into the city, for danger could scarcely come from any direction but the exterior. The deputies of the district chiefs also had the responsibility, at nightfall or shortly afterward, of closing the gates which isolated the quarters from each other and of not reopening them until the next day at dawn, and of making nocturnal rounds in the dark and deserted streets.

There was in Fez a state prison; it was located in the massive towers of the Gate of the Lion, near the palace of Fez Jdid. It was there that an infante of Portugal was imprisoned for several years in the fifteenth century, awaiting a liberation that did not come, and finally died. But only prisoners of note were confined there. The old city was provided with one prison, and probably even with two—one for men, the other for women. They were located not far from the residence of the governor and could, it is said, hold up to three thousand persons.

In Fez, the idea of prison evokes immediately that of hospital, at least of one hospital that is known to have been built or rebuilt in the Marinide period, and perhaps of others in the fourteenth century. It must be understood that the concept of a hospital in fourteenth-century Morocco had little in common with our present-day idea. In this period, a sick person normally did not go to a hospital: he was cared for at home and his family would have considered it shameful to send him away under the pretext that he was ill. The hospital served therefore only for the ill who had no one to take care of them—and these were rare—or else for the sick whom it was impossible to keep at home, the dangerously insane. It is immediately apparent why the idea of prison is linked with that of hospital. The hospital of Fez, given the name of an obscure saint called Sidi Frej, was divided into cells arranged around a courtyard. From the peak of the building's roof hung iron chains terminating at each cell and serving to keep quiet the unfortunate patients confined there, who, at least in the beginning, when they still had enough strength for it, spent part of their time screaming. According to Leo Africanus, who was secretary there for two years at the beginning of the sixteenth century, the sick lived in a deplorable state of filth in spite of the numerous personnel who had charge of them: these insane discouraged the best efforts and intentions.

The leprosarium, situated outside the ramparts, was also a sort of prison, but certainly less barbarous. Nothing definite is known about this institution.

There remain to be examined the services which maintained communications within Fez: first of all the public criers. Of course the sovereign and the governor could have notices read during the course of the Friday prayer, attended by a large part of the male population; this was always the case when communications of some length were disclosed. But at times the authorities might need to make known quickly to the public an order or a brief notice. They then had recourse to the public criers. The latter all had another trade, for that of crier would not have supported them. If what was stated later on is trustworthy, several of them were undertakers' employees, another occupation which does not fill every day, or sellers at public auction. One of them kept an office near the Sidi Frej hospital, almost in the center of the city, and could be found there at any hour of the day, whether it was a question of a corpse to be interred or an official notice to be brought to the attention of the public. In the latter case, the available criers were immediately called in: they learned the text of the message to be proclaimed, committed it to memory, and dispersed throughout the city, according to itineraries which were always the same, with stopping points in the most frequented spots so that the greatest number of people might be reached.

But disseminating news was not the only necessity; objects and merchandise also had to be circulated, and this was the task of the street porters and ass drivers. It has already been mentioned that the porters, or *zerzaya*, were and still are Berbers hailing from a few tribes of the middle valley of the Moulouya and the high valley of the Guir, numbering about three hundred. Their presence in Fez would date from the founding of the city, or almost so. From the sixteenth century on, and certainly earlier, they formed a close corporation because of the tribal and often family bonds which united them. They put their earnings in common and shared them at the end of each week. As they might be needed anywhere at any moment, they were distributed among a certain number of posts, analogous to taxi stands, whose importance varied according to the location. These posts were about fifteen in number at the beginning of the twentieth century, all situated on the Kairwanian Bank and, for the most part, toward the center of the city. As it is a question of an ancient organization with solid traditions, it may be inferred that the fourteenth-century organization was already as described, or nearly so. They were ready to carry the most diverse loads, sometimes very heavy, and were equipped for this purpose with sacks, so as not to wear out their clothing, and with ropes for stowing the packs. But they could sometimes be seen circulating without anything on their backs: they were then doing an errand or carrying a message, for they served as messengers as well as porters. Also they occasionally rented a horse or a mule when the load to be carried exceeded their strength. However, in general, transportation by beasts of burden was reserved for those called the "ass drivers," although they also used horses and mules.

These were contractors who had bought a few pack animals and rented them for the transportation of the various kinds of merchandise: boards or thick planks of cedar or olive wood used by carpenters or building contractors, loads of sand or brick needed for construction purposes, sacks of wheat or wool, and so forth. Thus little caravans of five or six donkeys, followed by a nonchalant ass driver, could be seen winding their way through the narrow streets of the city. As for mules and horses, each had a driver who led it by the bridle or else maintained in balance on its back a load difficult to secure. When two caravans of loaded animals encountered each other, it was sometimes difficult to pass—a blockage occurred, the drivers insulted each other and often the passers-by took part, then they ended by clearing the way and the animals continued on to their destination, or as far as the next obstruction. Without the infantry of porters and the cavalry of ass drivers, Fez could not have carried on its daily life, just as a modern city has great difficulty in getting along without trucks and public transportation.

The administration of religious properties and the witness-notaries may be said to constitute two other public services. Properties set apart for the pious foundations were, in fact, important; they included real estate situated in the city, such as the public baths, a large number of shops and warehouses, private dwellings, but also real property located in the country, sometimes at some distance from Fez. There was consequently the necessity of administering all of these holdings, of renting or designating the properties that could be rented, of making the indispensable repairs, of collecting rents or payments, of paying the anticipated expenses, of keeping the accounts of all these operations. Leo Africanus, at the beginning of the sixteenth century, speaks of thirty-five persons employed at these various tasks. This is certainly a minimum. Under the supervision of the cadi, this personnel was directed by a well-paid functionary; his was a heavy responsibility. The religious properties were divided into several sections, according to their destined use. The most important section managed the properties set aside for the Mosque of the Kairwanians. Then came the properties set apart for the hospital services, for Fez Jdid, and for diverse uses. The principal officials of this administration were scholars and belonged to the middle class of the city.

As to the notaries, they were assistants of the cadi, and in charge of procedure. Their instrumentality was indispensable for the majority of juridical acts of private life and of public life as well. They numbered around 160 at the beginning of the sixteenth century, and this figure must not have been very different from that of the fourteenth century, if it differed from it at all. Some were itinerant notaries who went to draw up documents on the premises; the majority remained in the shops along one of the façades of the Mosque of the Kairwanians. There they received their clients and drew up their instruments. All of them were, naturally, learned men who had been educated in Fez and knew not only the law but also the particular customs and the principal families of Fez; almost all were natives of the city and belonged to families of the middle class, for the inhabitants of the city would have been averse to confiding their interests to unknown persons or newcomers.

Lastly, to this brief list may be added the agents of financial services, for the religious properties were not, after all, the only ones to swell the resources of the city; the greater part of the merchandise entering the city was subject to a tax which varied according to the articles; there were also taxes on animals brought to the slaughterhouse. A functionary was accountable for all such taxes— or rather a farmer-general of revenues, who paid into the treasury a fixed daily amount, whatever might be the proceeds of his collections. He placed guards and secretaries at the gates, and sometimes sent agents out over the roads to some distance from the city in order to prevent fraud.

The modern reader will probably be surprised by the slight character of this community organization: a handful of officials, a small number of public services employing few persons, no visible participation of the citizens in the administration of the city, except by way of the experts from the trade corporations and the notables of the quarters, who participated actively in the nomination, and, in case of necessity, the dismissal of district heads. All this is surprising in connection with a populous city with several centuries of growth behind it, and settled by a well-established middle class. This situation is explained by the fact that Fez was a Moslem city; in the fourteenth century a Moslem city, whether located in Spain or Mesopotamia, was not administered according to any other norms. From this point of view, Moslem civilization borrowed almost nothing from Greek and Roman civilizations, one of whose distinctive characteristics was the expanding development of municipal life. On the other hand, the idea must be stressed that, however slight this organization may appear to us, it sufficed without the least doubt for the people of Fez. The settling of Fez was stable; granted, the population appears to have increased in the Marinide period, as is proved by the suburbs established outside the walls. It does not seem however that this increase in population was sudden or important. And it may well be questioned to what extent the suburban dwellers remained outside the city because they did not find any room in it. Perhaps it was rather because they did not have sufficient resources to establish themselves there and the community of Fez did nothing to help them. This suggests the idea of a closed society which lived a great deal to itself, and where everyone was acquainted, at least inside the same quarter. From this fact administration, indispensable when an anonymous mass of people is concerned, loses much of its reason for existence: no need for officials to search for or summon an individual; alerting an inhabitant of the quarter suffices and the errand will be done. No need for services of assistance and charity, for the ill or unfortunate individual always has relatives or friends who will help him, because this is their incontestable duty. In short, in a city like Fez in the fourteenth century, little basic groups, such as the family, the trade corporations, and in case of necessity, the immediate neighbors, are there to render to each one the services that the anonymous modern individual expects from the municipal administration. Community life did indeed exist, but it was fragmented into a great number of elementary cells.

IV

DAILY LIFE

It is possible to speak with certainty about the Marinide houses of Fez, for several of them have endured to our day. In the time of the Marinides, as today, there were different types of dwellings, according to the wealth of the proprietors; it is neither the poorest nor the simplest that have lasted up to the present. The ones known to us are the residences of families in comfortable circumstances; it should not be forgotten, however, that there were a number of such families in Fez, and that consequently the type of house known to us it not exceptional.

On the street side of these houses, there is a wall without other openings than several dormer windows through which it is possible to see what is happening in the street without the risk of being seen, and a solid wooden door, often ornamented by a pattern of nailheads in relief and a knocker with which the visitor announces his presence. Once the door is open, entrance is almost always into a corridor so bent and narrow that it is impossible to see from the threshold what is happening in the courtyard: the women thus have time to conceal their presence as soon as a stranger enters the door. The corridor leads to a courtyard, the patio, generally square in form; this courtyard is floored with marble slabs or with glazed faïence tiling, most often multicolored. In the center there may be a pool or a fountain of running water, or else the water arrives in a fountain located on the blind wall of the court. In fact, of the four walls which surround the courtyard, most often only three admit to rooms and openings; the fourth is blind and is generally a party wall. The three other inner sides of the court consist of covered galleries which allow passage from one room to another without danger of getting wet in case of bad weather. The rooms open on these galleries; there are three of them to a floor, each covering the length of one inner wall. The house often includes a ground floor and one upper story, sometimes two; the majority of the humble homes must have had only a ground floor. The galleries are supported by columns, square in many cases, whose base may be covered with multicolored faïence tiling up to an average height of three feet; the top of the column swells out into a sort of capital which may be of carved wood or moulded stuccowork. These capitals support lintels of carved wood which run along the three occupied walls. When there is only one upper story, the gallery of the second story is supported by wooden beams carved or simply squared off. The width of the gallery varies from three to six feet according to the importance of the residence. In the center of each gallery is a large door which extends up the entire height, about thirteen feet on the average. On each side of the door there are two symmetrical windows; each room gets its light from the courtyard through this door and these two windows. If, by chance, there is a garden adjoining the house—a luxury scarcely ever found except in the quarters near the periphery—one or two windows facing on this garden may be cut into the wall of the room opposite the entrance. It is possible, if the house is built on a steep slope, as often happens in Fez, that the party wall is not very high because the neighboring house is on a lower level, and from the gallery of the upper story a panorama of roofs and hills may be visible. But most frequently, even from the upper floor, the rooms look only into the patio.

A house with ground floor and one upper story includes six principal rooms, three to a floor. Kitchen, stairs, privies, lumber rooms are generally laid out in a blind corner; these are dead spaces and poorly lighted by dormer windows. The entire length of each room is, on the average, twenty-two to twenty-six feet, and the width hardly exceeds ten feet because the beams of the ceiling cannot be extremely long. Opposite the door, in the wall at the back of the room, there is often contrived a sort of alcove in brickwork which gives a little more depth to the center of the room. At the two ends are masonry benches whose lower part is hollow and can serve as a wardrobe. On these benches are beds. The floor is made of faïence tiling, as is often the lower part of the walls; the rest of the wall is whitewashed. In the luxurious homes the joists are of carved or painted wood; in the others they are of wood simply squared off. The furnishings consist of mattresses, covered with embroidered materials, and of cushions, which run along the walls. The floor may be covered by mats or by carpets. The house is roofed by a terrace built above the rooms of the upper floor and surrounded by rather high walls. Sometimes a slight structure rises from a corner of the terrace: it is a sort of belvedere from which can be contemplated a corner of the panorama of Fez. The terrace serves as an area for drying laundry, fruits, and vegetables, but it is first of all the domain of the women, who can go there to enjoy fresh air and sunshine and chat with the women of the neighboring houses. A small ladder is often seen there; this permits the women to clear the partition wall and visit their neighbors on the adjoining terraces, and, since many houses of Fez span the streets with archways, it is possible to go from terrace to terrace for several hundred yards, if one does a few gymnastics and is acquainted with a sufficient number of families.

A Fez house is therefore a space as carefully closed in as possible and turned entirely toward the patio; communication with the outside takes place only by way of the street door and the terraces. Each house is occupied by one family whose composition, naturally, is varied, but which generally includes the head of the family with his wife or wives, the married or unmarried sons to the extent of the available rooms, occasionally an old male or female relative, one or two female attendants, and sometimes slaves, according to the wealth of the household. In principle, each couple has at its disposal a room where parents and children sleep. The largest of the ground floor rooms serves as a reception hall, but that does not mean that it does not also serve as a bedroom once evening has come. A house with six rooms can thus shelter an average of about twenty persons. Poor families are not as luxuriously lodged; they get along with one or two rooms and share the premises with other families; in that case patio, terrace, kitchen, and privy are used in common. Such is the general framework in which the inhabitants of Fez lived. A luxurious dwelling may include several groups of buildings constructed around two or three patios communicating with each other, and even a private bath; the number of servants increases in proportion to the importance of the dwelling. The groups of buildings are sometimes arranged around an interior garden in which grow flowers, fruit trees, cypresses, an occasional palm tree; the clumps of trees are at a lower level, surrounded by walks paved with faïence tiles. However, this type of house is found only in the quarters around the periphery and never in the center of the city.

The population of Fez did not consist altogether of families; solitary men were numerous there—travelers or seasonal workers. Some of them found lodging with friends, or, in the case of workmen, on the premises where they worked. The poorest travelers could find asylum for the night in a mosque or in the buildings surrounding a saint's tomb. Many, however, had recourse to hostelries, numerous in Fez in the Middle Ages, if the account of Leo Africanus is credible. This author declares, in fact, that there were about 100 of them, some including up to 120 rooms and more. These were inns situated in the center of the city in the neighborhood of the Mosque of the Kairwanians, in the very center of business. He adds that the innkeepers formed an influential corporation. It was possible to eat in the inns, but on condition of preparing one's own food, for no meals were served there. In addition, the furnishings were rudimentary: the innkeeper provided his guests with a mat and a cover, nothing more. Lastly, in certain of these inns at least, the moral tone was highly questionable: traffic in wine was carried on there; it was a meeting place for women and men of doubtful morals. There was a marked contrast between the austere morality professed by the middle class of the city and these establishments, frequented chiefly, it is true, by strangers.

The people of Fez generally took three meals a day: the first, early in the morning after the dawn prayer, was composed of bread, fruit, and a gruel more substantial in winter than in summer; the second, after the noon prayer, was rather light in winter, more solid in summer, because meals were further apart; the third, between the sunset and the night prayers. There was a large consumption of bread, made at home and baked in the oven of the quarter; or couscous and semolina rolled into fine grains and cooked with steam. Milk was also a large part of the diet, in the form of fresh milk, curds, butter, or cheese. This milk was supplied to Fez by the peasants of the neighboring countryside, but also by several herds of cows which spent the night in stables in the city, close to the ramparts, and grazed all day around the outskirts. Fruits and vegetables, notably carrots and turnips, were abundant, coming from gardens located within the walls, or from the immediate countryside. Meat did not figure every day—far from it—in the menu of poor people; the middle class people consumed a great deal more of it; it consisted of mutton, sometimes goat meat, beef, and also poultry—chicken, pigeon, and, after the discovery of America, turkey. River fish was eaten also, chiefly shad, caught in the Sebou all winter long, from October to April. No detailed information is available concerning the fashion of preparing these dishes except in the case of mutton; it was stewed in a closed vessel, and the head was considered a particular delicacy. It may be supposed, however, that the cuisine of Fez was about what it was at the beginning of the twentieth century, with the exception of a few details, for its recipes seem to belong to an ancient tradition, partly of Andalusian origin. It must consequently have been varied and succulent, at least in many middle class families. Meals were taken in common around a low table; the guests squatted around the table, often on cushions, and served themselves directly from the platter with their right hands. Hands were carefully washed before and after the meal, and the mouth was rinsed out at the end of the repast. However different it might have been from the European custom, even at that period, this fashion of taking food followed a completely established etiquette and decorum. In general, the men of the house took their meals together, the women in another room; this rule was absolute when there was a guest in the house.

The articles of clothing were not very different from those described by European travelers of the eighteenth and nineteenth centuries; remarkable sketches of them are to be found in the travel albums of the painter Delacroix, who accompanied a French diplomatic mission at the beginning of the nineteenth century. Here are the descriptions given by Leo Africanus, at the beginning of the sixteenth century, concerning the clothing of the different social classes. First of all the middle class: "In the winter they wear garments of foreign-made cloth. Their costume is composed of a very close fitting short jacket, with half-sleeves, put on over the shirt. On top of this jacket, they wear a loose robe, with stitched front. And on top of that they put a burnoose. On their heads they wear a cap like some of those worn at night in Italy, but without ear flaps. On top of these caps they place a turban of rolled cloth which goes twice around the skull and passes under the chin. They wear neither stockings nor trunk hose, but they have cloth trousers. When they want to ride horseback in winter, they wear ankle boots. Men of the lower class wear the jacket and the burnoose but without the robe that has been mentioned, and on their heads they wear nothing besides one of these caps of no value. Doctors and elderly gentlemen are accustomed to wear widesleeved jackets like those of Venetian gentlemen, who hold the highest offices. Finally, men of the lowest class are dressed in white cloth made of coarse native wool; their burnoose is of the same material.

"The women are very well dressed, but in hot weather they wear only a shift that they draw in with a rather ugly belt. In the winter they put on wide-sleeved robes, stitched on the front like those of the men. When they go out, they wear trousers of such a length that the entire leg is covered, and a veil, after the manner of Syrian women, which covers their head and their whole body. The face likewise is covered with a piece of cloth so that they leave only the eyes exposed. In their ears they wear great rings of gold with very beautiful precious stones. They also have gold bracelets on their wrists, one on each arm, bracelets which may commonly weigh one hundred ducats (around three hundred fifty grams). Women who are not of the nobility have them made of silver, and they wear similar ones on their legs."

It may be inferred that the cloth used for making the outer garments was of different colors and that there existed fashions in clothing, changing and imperious modes.

The principal stages of family life were marriage, the birth of children, circumcision of the boys, and death. Leo Africanus—always he—furnishes in these matters information that is very definite, although sometimes requiring cautious acceptance.

Marriage was above all a family affair: it was not simply a man and a woman who were being united by the bonds of marriage, but also and chiefly, as in Europe of that time, two families. Consequently the marriage was arranged by the parents; the young man was consulted, the young girl informed, and rare were those who tried to go against the will of their parents, at least openly. Leo Africanus does not speak about the role of the female matchmakers in the conclusion of matrimonial unions; he mentions them only in describing the marriage ceremonies and speaks of them only as dressers. It is possible that this corporation of women, who were to exercise later on such a great influence on the society of Fez, played at that time only the role (after all secondary) of mistress of ceremonies. The marriage project, having been arranged in secret in one fashion or another, became public when the two fathers met in a mosque with their best friends and placed the future union under divine protection, at the same time that they had the marriage contract drawn up. This contract fixed the amount of the marriage portion to be paid by the husband and of the trousseau to be supplied by the girl; its conclusion was accompanied by reciprocal gifts. The value of the trousseau corresponded in general to the amount of the marriage portion, in conformity with the custom of Fez. In families of comfortable circumstances, or in those who wanted to appear so, the expenses thus agreed upon, to which were added the expenses of the marriage itself, reached considerable sums, and were a heavy burden. In middle class families at least, it was a tradition for marriages to take place at an early age; most young men were married before the age of twenty, girls before the age of fifteen. It even happened fairly often for a future husband and wife to be betrothed when they were still children. Engagements could therefore be of long duration.

When the two families had fixed the wedding date, preferably in the season of fine weather, for some of the ceremonies took place in the patios and were ill adapted to rain and cold, the bustle of the preparations began: laying in of supplies, invitations, arrangements with the women matchmakers or dressers, and the musicians. Finally began the festivities which lasted a week and took place simultaneously in the respective houses of the engaged couple.

The culminating point was the night when the affianced was conducted in procession from her house to that of her future husband; a cortege formed around the palanquin in which the betrothed girl took her place and which bearers carried on their shoulders, "an eight-sided coffer of wood covered with beautiful materials of silk and brocade." On the threshold of the nuptial chamber, the sumptuously dressed and abundantly made-up girl was welcomed by her husband; this was often their first meeting, unless, as frequently happened, they were cousins and had known each other in their childhood. The couple retired into a room specially prepared for them and the consummation of the marriage took place at that time; immediately afterward, the dresser on duty showed to the company assembled in the patio a blood-spotted cloth which bore witness to the fact that the girl was indeed a virgin. When the future wife remarried after widowhood or divorce, the ceremonies had much less pomp; they were much simpler also among the lower classes. It is known that Moslem law permits men to have as many as four legitimate wives, on condition they can assure them equal treatment, and also to divorce their wives without explanation or formal procedure. As a matter of fact, it seems that this was never the case in Fez: in this city of well-established families, divorce was frowned upon in practice, if not by law, and polygamy was not frequent; many marriage contracts stipulated that the man would not take any other wife, except in precisely specified cases, notably in the case of his wife's not giving him a child. Moslem law also tolerates the presence of concubines in addition to the legitimate wives, but there again the custom of Fez was more restrictive and concubines do not appear ever to have been numerous. It is possible that the stability of matrimonial unions was less great in the lower classes, in particular among the new citizens who had not yet become adapted to the customs of the city.

The birth of a child was always considered a happy event, but even more so if the child, especially the first-born, was a boy. Seven days after birth, the child received its baptismal name and this was an occasion of great family rejoicing. If it was a boy, he might be circumcised as early as a few days after birth, but the family often waited until he had reached the age of seven or eight years to arrange this ceremony. After the barber had performed the operation, the small boy was dressed in finery and led through the city on a mule. The rearing of the children during their first years was entirely in the hands of the women of the house: mother, grandmother, aunts, and servants. When the boy arrived at an age to begin his studies, his father took the responsibility of directing his education; the girls, who almost never went to school, remained under the rule of their mothers until their marriage, after which they passed under the authority of their husbands and in-laws, since in the majority of cases they went to live with the husband's family.

When a death occurred, the house was plunged into mourning—a contained and decorous mourning in the middle class families, an ostentatious mourning in the lower classes where the women tore their hair and bruised their faces, and where hired mourners, men or women, came to increase the lamentations. The body was carefully washed and sewed into a shroud, after which it was borne to the cemetery on a wooden litter; only the men accompanied the funeral procession, chanting pious litanies. Often they stopped en route at a mosque where, inside a special enclosure, they recited brief prayers for the repose of the deceased's soul. There were several private cemeteries in the middle of the city around the tomb of some well-known saint, but the majority of the cemeteries were located in the neighborhood of the ramparts, either inside or outside; the most important were situated near Bab Gisa to the north and Bab Ftuh to the south. In most cases, the body was laid directly in the earth, the face turned in the direction of Mecca; the tomb, in the case of a member of the middle class, was covered over with a flagstone which often took the form "of a long slender stone with a triangular back," sometimes artistically carved. At the head and foot of the tomb stood two slabs of marble on which were carved the name of the deceased, the date of his death, and often, pious inscriptions, occasional verse, or fragments of the Koran. Leo Africanus does not say whether, in the Marinide epoch, the women were accustomed to go to the cemetery on Friday afternoons, as was their habit later on. They went to pray, of course, but also to meet, gossip, and eat delicacies.

The daily life of the men was occupied by the duties of their profession, the administration of their property, if they had any, and the task of provisioning the household, for this responsibility fell to them since, at least in the middle class families, the women went out as little as possible. In fact, they spent the greater part of their time at home caring for the children and doing the household tasks, often also embroidering and, in the lower classes, spinning or sewing in order to make a little money. In bad weather, they stayed in the rooms inside the house, but, as soon as fine weather came, they remained ordinarily in the patio or on the terrace, especially at the end of the day, when the sun was not too strong. Then the terraces of Fez blossomed out with women in light-colored clothing who chatted from house to house, and often visited each other by climbing over the walls. The young engaged men profited by this moment to climb a hill near the city and, from there, tried to distinguish those who would become their wives. However, the women did go out from time to time, hermetically enveloped in veils, as has been mentioned earlier. In this way they went to visit their families, sometimes for two or three days; they visited their friends, took part in the family festivities to which they were invited, and also went regularly to the baths, at the hour which was reserved for them. Occasionally also, when their husbands permitted it, they went to the *Qisariya* in order to make purchases. Generally they did not go out alone, but were accompanied by a woman of the family or a maid servant. This life, more than half recluse, has often moved the Occidentals who have spoken of it to pity. But it must be remembered that the women of Fez scarcely suffered from it at all, because they did not imagine that any other life was possible, and they were perfectly accustomed to it. That did not prevent some of them from having amorous adventures, on condition of course that they were able to obtain some kind of complicity: maid servant, old understanding aunt, go-between—for these existed—or simply a neighbor on the next terrace. The number of these romantic adventures was probably limited, but not negligible.

The monotony of daily life was broken by a few amusements; the men played chess, at least in middle class circles, the women organized from time to time extemporaneous gatherings for dancing and singing. But above all there were the festivals; family festivals already mentioned, numerous in this city of a powerful middle class; public festivals too, in which the men participated in the streets while the women watched from the roof tops. The religious festivals and Ramadan, the month of fasting, which will be mentioned again later, were occasions for rejoicing. There were also the traditional festivals, certainly of pre-Islamic origin, such as the Saint John's fires in the month of June; and official festivities on the occasion of a victory obtained by the sovereign, a marriage at the court, an accession to the throne, the official entry of the sovereign into his capital upon his return from an expedition or a sojourn in another city, or simply on the occasion of a military parade. Here is how a fourteenth-century author describes one of these celebrations: "The men from each *suq* go out in a certain direction, each having a longbow or any other weapon, adorned in their finest clothing. The men of each *suq* spend that night outside the city. Each *suq* has a standard which is its distinctive sign, and which carries armorial bearings corresponding to each trade. Very early in the morning, when the sultan comes out, these men form lines and march in front of him. In the meantime he advances on horseback, having his guard on his right and on his left; the renegades surround him at the rear; the standards float at his right, and the drummers are behind him, until he celebrates the prayer. When he comes back, the men of the *suqs* return to their homes."

These popular festivals sometimes gave rise, in this period when games and sports did not exist, to rivalries—often violent—between young men of different quarters. Leo Africanus explains it in the following manner: "In certain periods of the year, the young men gather and those from one street, armed with cudgels, fight with those from another street. It sometimes happens that the adversaries get inflamed against one another to the point of taking up arms, and several kill each other, especially at the time of the festivals when the young men congregate outside of the city. After the mêlée is finished, they start throwing stones at one another, so that often the police commissioner who wants to separate them cannot succeed in doing so. But he arrests some of them and puts them in prison. These are then flogged through the city. At night many fire-eaters provided with weapons go together outside the city. They wander among the gardens and into the countryside. If they run into fire-eaters from an enemy street, a violent brawl breaks out, for these people always feel a mortal hatred for each other. But frequently they are severely chastised and punished for it." This is a relic, no doubt, of old racial tensions which had manifested themselves in the early years of Fez, when the city was inhabited by heterogeneous and poorly welded elements, and which still reappeared—even up to the beginning of the twentieth century—on certain occasions.

In addition to these extraordinary pleasures, the lower classes had frequent amusements which were not expensive. These were furnished by storytellers who installed themselves near the gates, in an open space located inside or outside the ramparts. Accompanied by a tabor and often by one or two stringed or wind instruments, they declaimed, with many a gesture, verses or sequences in rhymed prose which recounted the exploits or the loves of heroes of former times. They also sold amulets or talismans to add to their small earnings. Festival days were particularly favorable for them, but they also had visitors each time the weather was fine, toward the end of the day, since many workers were free after the midafternoon prayer. Other mountebanks exhibited monkeys and charmed serpents at the same time that they told fortunes by means of figures traced in the sand. It is probable that there were also troops of traveling acrobats who gave performances in the open air.

As for the middle class people, they often owned in the outer quarters of the city, and particularly in the sparsely built-up southern area, gardens of fruit trees, vegetables, and flowers. Often they had had built there little summer-houses where they and their families could take refreshment and rest sheltered from the sun, in the midst of the greenery and the birds and the murmur of running waters. They often went there in the season of fine weather, from April to October, and even at times took advantage of a few sunny winter days. Sometimes the family even slept there for several days. Meals were not prepared there but were brought from the family home, which was never very far away.

Fez offered also less respectable diversions, indulged in especially by bachelors, but which perhaps attracted others. Smokers of hashish, of whom Leo Africanus speaks several times, were to be found there; wine could also be obtained. The authorities closed their eyes in the matter, for the keepers of these questionable establishments did what was necessary to remain undisturbed. Prostitutes were chiefly established on the Andalusian Bank, under the surveillance of the *muhtasib*, responsible, it must be remembered, for watching over public morals. Lastly homosexuality, although violently condemned by Moslem law, and theoretically considered a shameful practice, was in fact tolerated to the extent that there existed male prostitutes, who dressed like women, wore the same jewels that they wore, were clean-shaven, adopted the feminine manner of speaking, and, exclaims Leo Africanus with horror, even pushed the resemblance to the point of spinning! No doubt the segregation of the sexes, even if it was not absolute, was the principal cause of this type of behavior.

All in all, however, it appears that Fez was a city of good morals. It was dominated by a strict middle class morality in its principles and was careful of appearances. This entailed a fair amount of hypocrisy, but a French moralist has said, not without sagacity, that hypocrisy is homage rendered by vice to virtue. In any tightly organized society, a certain amount of hypocrisy is indispensable, for it alone permits social life to maintain its course without too many hitches. The society of Fez was particularly close-knit. Its middle class of scholars, government officials, and businessmen set the general tone and conformed, in appearance at least, to the rigorous social etiquette which had been established little by little. The only ones who escaped it more or less were the newcomers to the city, those who had not yet had time to adapt to the local rules of social propriety. But they came to it by degrees and slowly melted into that society which was at least heedful of living according to convention.

Two communities led a life apart: the Jewish community and the court. The Jews were the only inhabitants of Fez who were not Moslems. There had probably been Christians there formerly, since one of the gates of Fez, on the Andalusian Bank, was still called the Gate of the Church, but they had long since disappeared, certainly since the Almohade period and probably well before that time. As for Christians coming from Europe, there were none in Fez in the fourteenth century, with the exception of some captives, taken prisoner at the time of military expeditions in Spain, and the Christian militia of the Suburb of the Christians in Fez Jdid, a military community about which we have no information for the period in question.

We have no precise information about the Jews of Fez in the fourteenth century, except that this community did exist, and that it was housed in the old city of Fez, probably concentrated in the quarter next to Bab Gisa. We know also that this community did not play any political role, since the historiographer of Abu'l-Hasan, Ibn Marzuq, praises his master for not having employed any Jew in the service of the state. It was not to be so in the following century: in the middle of the fifteenth century several wealthy Jews were to take on great importance and one of them was even to be the veritable master of the kingdom for several years, until he was overthrown by a popular revolt.

It is possible however to get an approximate idea of Jewry in Fez through what is known of the condition of Jews in general in the Moslem Occident of that period. They had been badly treated by the Almohades, but had regained their former status with the accession of the Marinides. They formed a community which enjoyed complete religious autonomy, on condition that the exercise of their worship would not disturb the Moslem population. Within the framework of this religious liberty, they had the right to regulate their affairs of personal status (marriage, inheritance, etc.) in conformity with the Mosaic law. There was therefore in Fez, as elsewhere, a corps of rabbis who directed the observances of worship, taught the Hebraic doctrine and law, and settled the disputes which arose within the community. As the number of Jews of that time is unknown, it is impossible to know what the importance of the rabbinical clergy was. Neither do we know what relations existed between the rabbis of Fez and those outside; it is probable that these contacts did not extend far and must scarcely have gone beyond Tlemcen on the east and Moslem Spain on the north. It is probable also that, from this period on, the Jewish community sent a representative to the Marinide government—a community leader, named by the government upon the recommendation of the community, thus analogous in many respects to the district chiefs and the heads of the trade corporations. This official was charged with transmitting to the government the wishes and grievances of the community, in the same way that he made known to his coreligionists the desires or the orders of the Moslem authorities. And lastly he was responsible for maintaining order within the community. He was probably in regular communication with the governor of Old Fez, to whom he was directly accountable.

It is impossible, always through lack of information, to give an exact idea of the manner in which the Jews lived. Many, according to all probability, pursued occupations of the handicraft type, since certain activities, as has been seen, were reserved for them in practice, if not by law. Others certainly devoted themselves to commerce, since some are known to have become extremely wealthy in the fifteenth century; this wealth certainly did not come to them from handicraft occupations which, as has been said, furnished a living but not a fortune. In addition since their right to acquire real property was extremely limited, if it even existed, they had not acquired their fortunes by way of speculation in real estate. Therefore it is impossible to see how anything but commerce could have permitted them to amass money.

And lastly, only conjectures are possible concerning their customs. It is probable that marriages between individuals belonging to the two different communities were rare; perhaps some Jewish girls married Moslems, but in that case they were converted and were lost to their community. The contrary must never have happened. Probably certain unions were concluded with Jews of other communities of Morocco and even of Spain, but they were undoubtedly rare and limited to the few truly wealthy families who had contacts with the outside. The general rule was certainly endogamy. It may also be inferred that customs, food, and clothing must have been analogous to what was usual in Moslem society, with this difference—the women certainly did not veil themselves when they went out. Did the men still wear the special costume that had been imposed upon them by the Almohade caliph al-Mansur at the end of the twelfth century? This is impossible to affrm or deny. What can be affirmed is that, in its over-all aspect, this community, surely small in numbers, lived peaceably and maintained good relations with the Moslems since no chronicler mentions a serious incident. It was only in the fifteenth century that incidents, concerning whose nature we have no exact information, but which must have been serious, led the Marinide government to install the Jews in the quarter of Homs in Fez Jdid, a quarter which was to take later on the name of Mellah. It is then only, when the Jewish community occupied a clearly separate place, that precise information about it begins to be available.

We are better informed concerning the court, described by several authors writing in Arabic. It led a life completely different from that of the old city. At the time of the Marinide conquest, it was primarily a Bedouin court, where the Marinide and Arabic chiefs, used to a warlike and nomadic existence, held the principal positions. Then the court became fixed to a certain extent, although it was still quite often nomadic, since the Marinide sovereigns had to organize many military expeditions and, even in times of peace, frequently toured their kingdom in order to be seen, to levy taxes, and to maintain their authority. The sovereign had to appear in all of the provinces of the kingdom at regular intervals and this tradition has been maintained up to the present time. While he was scouring the country, Fez Jdid was a more than half-empty city, where troops were few in number, and where a part of the royal family lived, surrounded by the indispensable servants. The high officials of the kingdom often accompanied the king on these expeditions and also left their residences half empty.

But when the sovereign returned to settle down in his capital, it filled up again with great numbers of soldiers, servants, and functionaries, and took on new life. However, the life of the court did not resemble that of the old middle class city of Fez; it was dominated by an official hierarchy that no one could transgress. At the summit of the pyramid reigned the sovereign upon whom all depended, small things as well as great. Below him came the ministers who were only his servants, but servants of high rank, to whom all the others owed respect, the military chiefs, and the principal functionaries, who were generally members of the Marinide tribe and of the principal Arabic tribes which relied on the dynasty. There must also be taken into account the members of the royal family who frequently had no occupation, because the king did not want to give them any real powers that they might have been able to use against him, but who naturally received great honors. Women played no official role in this court, since the rule of the separation of sexes forbade their appearing in public. This does not mean that they had neither role nor influence, but only that they played their part in secret. These women were numerous; they might include the mother of the sovereign, sometimes his grandmother, his legitimate wives and his concubines, who were often Christian captives, especially Spanish or Portuguese women, or black slaves. Finally, the lowest rank of the court was made up of servants, for the most part slaves or freedmen, among whom existed a hierarchy and fierce jealousy. Often the sovereign singled out one or another of his servants in order to make him a high official—those who were directly attached to his personal service had the greatest chance of being so honored. It is easy to imagine the permanent atmosphere of intrigue which must have prevailed at this court, as around all the great of the world.

We have some information about the daily life of the court, furnished by a few Arabic authors of the fourteenth century, and by Leo Africanus in the sixteenth. They are all agreed that Abu'l-Hasan and Abu 'Inan began their day early with the dawn prayer. Then took place in the presence of the sovereign an assembly of scholars, which the traveler Ibn Batuta, who was in Fez in 1349, describes in the following way: "Our master holds scholarly assemblies every day after the dawn prayer in the mosque of his illustrious palace; the princes of the jurisconsults and the most distinguished of their disciples attend. Before the sovereign is read the commentary of the noble Koran, the tradition of the Prophet chosen by God—through him prayer and salvation—works relative to the doctrine of Malik [head of the juridical school to which Morocco adhered] and books of the mystics. In all these phases of learning, our master holds the first rank. . . . Among all the other kings of the earth, I have never known a one whose solicitude for learning attained such a high degree."

An Egyptian chronicler of the same period furnishes some supplementary details: "The sultan has the custom of holding audience every day at an early hour. The great shaykhs come there to greet him: these are the ones who at his court hold the rank of emirs of *tûman* in Iran, and of commanders of a thousand men in Egypt. For them is served a repast consisting of bowls of broth, in front of which are dishes containing viands of all sorts, at the same time as sweets, some of which are made of sugar, but for the most part of honey; there are some of both kinds, but sugar is scarce and the majority of the sweets are made of honey mixed with oil. When those present have finished the meal, they disperse into their rooms."

Then the sultan sometimes rides horseback, but this is not always the case. On the other hand, at the end of the afternoon after the prayer, the sovereign rides out and attends military exercises: "He remains standing on a little rise of ground; troops mount horse around him; in front of him the horses rush against one another; the horsemen tilt with their lances, adversaries challenge each other. They are imitating war in front of him; their close-packed ranks maneuver before him as if this were truly war and combat, and all that with the aim of training for war. Then, with his royal escort, he returns to his palace; the men-at-arms disperse into their lodgings and the doctors, the men of great attainments, and the important personages are brought in to keep him company during the night. A tablecloth is spread out before him and he has his guests served with food. Thereupon the secretary of state has a private interview with him to settle affairs, to examine petitions and lists of claims. These personages spend with the sultan the greater part of the nights, save for the secretary of state to whom he gives, on certain evenings, the order to spend the night in the palace, and who, in that case, remains there in a private apartment."

The sovereign is not content with directing the affairs of state, he devotes a certain time to the examination of the private cases presented to him by his subjects: "For the audience in which he judges the complaints of his subjects, the sultan presides on carpets heaped up in a pavilion reserved for these audiences. Sometimes he sits on a throne which is only slightly elevated; sometimes he sits on a mat; and in his presence the shaykhs sit down, girded with their sabers. When a plaintiff wishes to bring his complaint to the attention of the sultan, this is possible only at the moment when the latter is on horseback and appears in public; he shouts to the sultan from a distance: 'There is no God but Allah, aid me, Allah will aid thee.' The sultan learns in this way that there is a complaint to be presented; his petition is taken from him and is remitted to the secretary of state. When the sultan returns to his palace, he keeps with him the secretary of state, who reads to him this petition and others; he then makes decisions in the matter." Ibn Batuta, who saw these things with his own eyes, gives the following slightly different version: "The sovereign has the habit of holding audiences expressly for the purpose of listening to the complaints of his subjects. He devotes Friday to the poor; he divides this day between the men and the women, having the latter appear first because of their weakness. The petitions of the women are read after the Friday prayer [the noon prayer] and up to the time of the afternoon prayer. Each woman is called in turn by her name; she remains standing in the noble presence of the sultan who speaks to her without intermediary. If she has been unjustly treated, redress comes without delay; if she asks a favor, this is quickly granted. After the afternoon prayer has been performed, cognizance is taken of the men's petitions and the sovereign deals with these in the same way as with the women's. The jurisconsults and the cadis are present at the audience and the sultan refers to them everything connected with prescriptions of the law. This is a procedure that I have never seen employed in a manner so perfect, with so much equity, by any sovereign; for the king of India has charged one of his emirs with the function of receiving the petitions from the hands of the public, with drawing up a succinct report and setting it forth to the sovereign; but the latter does not have the plaintiffs or the petitioners appear before him."

At times also the sultan appeared in public, on the occasion of the religious festivals or of some extraordinary event; he never did it other than on horseback and according to an immutable ceremonial described by Leo Africanus: "When the king wishes to mount horse, the master of ceremonies informs the couriers of it in his name. The latter then apprise the relatives of the king, the captains, the wardens, and the other horsemen. They all assemble in the square in front of the palace and in the neighboring streets. When the king comes out of the palace, the couriers oversee the orderly formation of the procession. The standard bearers march at the head followed by the kettledrummers. Then comes the master of the stables, with his subordinates and his favorites, then the bursar with his group; then the wardens; then the master of ceremonies, then the king's secretaries, the treasurer, the judge, and the captain of the army. The king comes next, accompanied by the grand counselor and by some prince. Certain officers on horseback precede the king: one bears his sword, another his shield, and another his crossbow. Around him march his livery servants, one of whom carries his halberd, another the saddle covering and the halter of his horse; when he dismounts, this covering is spread over the saddle and the halter passed over the bridle, in order to lead the horse by hand. Another livery servant carries the king's pattens, wooden footwear decorated with beautiful embellishments and which are objects for pomp and ostentation. The chief of the livery servants comes behind the king. He is followed by the eunuchs. After that the procession includes the king's family, followed by the light cavalry, then the crossbowmen and the arquebusiers. The costume worn by the king on this occasion is modest and correct. Anyone not acquainted with the king does not think that it could be he, for his livery servants are more lavishly dressed than he, with rich and ornamented materials. No king, no Mohammedan lord wears on his head a crown or anything at all resembling it, because the law of Mohammed forbids it."

The last-mentioned trait should be noted: the simplicity practiced by the sovereign in his manner of dress, in such marked contrast to the luxury of the Mamelukes and, later on, of the Ottoman Empire. This may be viewed as a relic of the Bedouin origins of the Marinide dynasty, but it may also be thought of as a trait of Berber austerity; this country tolerates ostentatious display, but does not take part in it directly, and the Marinide sovereign gives the example of this reserve.

V

ECONOMIC ACTIVITY

IF TRADITION IS TRUSTWORTHY, Fez has at all times been a city of business, a great commercial and industrial center. Whatever may be the value of this assertion in connection with the Idrisside era, it is interesting to note that it is justifiably set forth by chroniclers of the first years of the fourteenth century, that is to say, within about twenty years of the period under consideration. For men writing at that moment and probably not having at their disposition numerous documents concerning the early history of the city, the intense economic activity they witnessed seemed to them so thoroughly ingrained in the essential nature of Fez that they could not imagine the city otherwise occupied than in manufacturing and selling. They quite naturally projected into the past what was going on under their eyes. If we had no other evidence than this, it would still be important and significant.

Fez was, therefore, an industrial city. It must not be forgotten that this was a medieval industry, having little connection with what is now understood by this word, except for the fact that industry, starting with a raw material—animal, vegetable or mineral—transforms it into articles fit for daily consumption or use; this is just as true in the case of a tanner of Fez as in that of an automobile factory in Detroit.

A complete lack of documents makes it impossible to

give any precise details on the rate—rapid or slow—of industrial development in Fez. Only a glimpse may be caught of the fact that it was early enlivened by the bringing in of specialists from the outside, with the tested techniques of old city dwellers. We know, in fact, that in the first quarter of the ninth century, shortly after its founding, Fez received successively two groups of citizens driven out of Córdoba and Kairwan for political reasons. It is known that, among the Córdobans at least, there were numerous artisans. Thus there were Kairwanian techniques, that is to say Oriental, with perhaps a few traces of Byzantine influence; Córdoban techniques, Oriental also in basis, but penetrated by Latin and Iberic influences; and Berber techniques undoubtedly, for the major part of the population of Fez was Berber in the beginning. How did these techniques adapt to one another? How did they evolve and what did they produce up to the time when the Almoravides revived the Spanish influence in Fez by bringing there numerous specialists of Peninsular origin? The absence of archeological documents permits no reply. From the moment these documents do exist, that is to say, from the Almoravide era, it can be affirmed that the handicraft techniques of Fez were profoundly marked by Andalusian influence. They were to remain so up to the time of the Marinides and well beyond. It can also be affirmed that the industrial impetus of Fez dates at the latest from the Almoravide period; it probably went on increasing up to the fourteenth century, for there is no reason to think that it experienced any serious abatement.

In the city of Abu'l-Hasan and Abu 'Inan some one hundred fifty corporations worked side by side, filling certain quarters with a clamour of implements striking in rhythm, with slapping of leather, with rustling of fabrics, and with voices of men giving orders, arguing or singing. Thus, a sort of symphony of toil welled up every day out of the valley of Fez.

The majority of these artisans worked primarily for their fellow citizens, for Fez consumed the greater part of what it produced; this was particularly the case with foodstuffs. Three principal groups of workers satisfied the alimentary needs of Fez: millers, oven-keepers, and oilmakers. The millers were established all along the river and its branches, and their mills, about four hundred in number at the beginning of the sixteenth century, operated without difficulty thanks to the steep slope characteristic of Fez—a drop of more than two hundred feet in level between the river's entrance into the city and its exit, say a distance of about five-eighths of a mile. Most of the time the millers worked with the customers' own grain: each one brought them something to be ground, some one sack, some ten sacks, of wheat or barley; it was almost unheardof for them to buy grain themselves and sell the flour already prepared.

In order to designate those who baked the bread, the language of Fez did not use the term "bread kneaders," and this was right, for these workmen did not make the bread, they confined themselves to baking it. Each family made its own bread and carried it each morning to the nearest oven or the one with the most thriving business: each ball was stamped with a distinguishing mark so as to avoid confusion. At the hour when the baking was finished, the oven was assailed by a band of children, servants, or women impatiently waiting, chattering and arguing, to carry away quickly the round, hot, golden loaves.

The olive oil mills were all located near the two gates through which the loads of olives arrived—Bab Gisa and

Bab Ftuh—but the most numerous were situated near Bab Gisa, along the ramparts, because the olive groves were more numerous on the hills which extended to the north of the city, as far as the Sebou River, then on to the Wargha River and beyond, on the first slopes of the mountains which bordered the Mediterranean. This industry worked only a few months out of the year, just long enough to handle the harvest, and, for that reason, it appealed to a group of seasonal workers who arrived from the north at the same time as the olives. This worked out well since, aside from the plowing, the work of the oil mills was done in the slack agricultural season. The equipment was rudimentary: a courtyard in whose center rose a stone trough where the olives were crushed under a millstone, turned by an animal which went tirelessly round and round the whole day long. The paste thus obtained, and from which a first oil had already been pressed, was then introduced into flat two-handled esparto baskets that were carried to the press: an old wooden framework, a wide plank of olivewood, and a rustic press screw, also of olivewood. Having taken refuge near the walls, in rarely frequented quarters, the oil mills ran little risk of annoying the population by their filth: at the most a few traces of oil and an acrid odor in the streets where transportation of the raw material and the finished product took place.

In addition to these three fundamental industries the service of food supply of Fez sustained no other industries, but a few small trades that must be mentioned, and first of all the corporation of the butchers, established principally near the center of the Kairwanian Bank, but with annexes in the main quarters, and in particular on the Andalusian Bank—about forty shops in all. The slaughterhouse was situated downstream from the last bridge, quite near where the river emerged from the city. Mutton was eaten by preference, then beef, then goat meat, and finally, as a supplement and in the poor quarters, camel meat when any was available. As for poultry, it was always bought alive from special merchants, fattened and killed at home, as was the sheep of the Feast of the Sacrifice. In the spring, several butchers, and sometimes tanners, were employed by private individuals of considerable means to prepare the preserved meats used in winter or in case of an impromptu meal. There were to be found also in Fez numerous proprietors of cheap cookshops in which were fed persons without families or transient travelers, dealers in roast beans, sausages, various fried foods, fritters, sweets and pastries. The latter had also the people of the town as customers. They must have been relatively numerous, particularly around the approaches to the city gates.

Many workmen were employed by the different trades which co-operated in the construction of public or private buildings. Naturally we do not have at hand statistics on the activity of the building trades under the Marinides, but we have the tangible proof that it was considerable, since it is possible to date from the Marinide period, sometimes with the greatest precision, a large number of mosques, schools, private homes, and the whole city of Fez Jdid, with its fortifications, which was the work of the laborers of the old city.

The equivalent of our architects and our building contractors could not be found in Fez. When buildings constructed at state expense were concerned, it is probable that certain functionaries of the central administration had little by little become specialists in construction problems and assumed the office of engineers: certain chronicles speak of the engineers (*muhandisin*) who perfected the plans of Fez Jdid. Private individuals, who did not have the same means as the state, drew up themselves a rough plan of what they wanted, taking into account their needs, the form, the area, and the nature of the building site, then addressed themselves to the different trade corporations concerned, discussed with them the work to be done and the price to be paid, and themselves supervised the construction work once it was under way.

It is possible to distinguish the trade corporations whose principal task was to furnish materials which were often utilized by others. Such were the brickmakers; the different categories of potters who produced the conduits for the conveyance and evacuation of water, the roofing tiles, and the glazed tiles which served for paving the courtyards, flooring the rooms, and facing the lower part of the walls; the limemakers, whose ovens were almost all located on the hills situated to the north of the city, quite close to the raw material; the carpenters who prepared the beams for the ceilings and roofs, when there were any —cedar beams for the most part, but sometimes olivewood; the smiths who made the window grills and the locks; and lastly the marble cutters, whom the wealthy people charged with lining basins and pools, and sometimes with flagging the courtyards. Marble was found not far from Fez, on the slopes of the Middle Atlas, but those who had great wealth had marble imported from Spain or from Italy, and sometimes already cut and polished.

Clothing industries were flourishing because, with the exception of a few quite costly fabrics imported from Europe or the Orient, everything that the inhabitants wore was produced locally.

The weavers were subdivided into several corporations according to the material that they handled: wools of different qualities, cotton, silk, flax. Certain of them used rather rudimentary looms to weave the hooded cloaks of coarse wool which were primarily sold to the peasants of the surrounding countryside. Others used more and more complicated looms to weave the fabrics used by the city dwellers, from plain-colored ordinary wool to silk with flowered patterns. In the sixteenth century, Fez counted more than five hundred ateliers of weavers, employing up to twenty thousand persons. There is every reason to believe that this industry was already as flourishing in the fourteenth century; it was the most important one of Fez and, though it produced products for export into other Moroccan cities and even abroad, a large part of its output was used locally. The weavers furnished work for several other trade corporations which prepared their raw material for them; in particular the spinners, poor women who worked at home, and the dyers established along the river in the neighborhood of the bridge which bore their name, the Bridge of the Dyers. They made use of coloring materials of mineral origin, which were to be found near the city and which were ground up, like those used by the potters, in a few specialized mills.

The tanners constituted another important corporation who dressed the hides of sheep, goats, oxen, and, in addition, camels and gazelles. They formed four groups who seemed to have specialized early in the tanning of the different skins mentioned above. If we add to the tanners a few corporations who worked only for them, such as the dehairers who removed the hair from the skins, the millers who pulverized the different raw materials employed in tanning, and the leather dyers, the workers specializing in the preparation of leather may be estimated at about one thousand.

Once it was tanned, the leather passed into the hands of different guilds who made various articles from it. There were the harness makers and the saddle makers who made the harness for beasts of burden and riding animals; the makers of leather bags, the bookbinders, and above all, the shoemakers who furnished the inhabitants of Fez and the surrounding region with boots, footwear, and list slippers. When decorated articles were concerned, the embroiderers, women of humble or average station who worked at home, then entered the field. Granting that a good part of the population went barefoot, the corporation of the shoemakers was nevertheless an important one; it employed several hundred workmen. To it must be added the humble corporation of the cobblers who repaired worn footwear, and those who made the wooden pattens which the middle class used in case of bad weather.

Fabrics produced locally could be made up at home, as was the case in poor families where the women sewed the clothing of the household. But people of means had recourse to tailors or dressmakers. The tailors worked in close conjunction with the lacemakers and with beltmakers, who furnished men as well as women with embroidered belts; the embroidery work was done by women at home, just as was the embroidery on leather.

Lastly, artisans who came from Spain had created in Fez the industry of making headgear, those skull caps of red felt, stiff or soft, often called in Europe "fez" because of the place in which they were made, but which in their place of origin are called *shashiya* or *tarbush*.

It was necessary also to manufacture locally the stock of tools required for all the industrial activities and for the everyday domestic activities, since at that time little was imported. Blacksmiths made the metal tools used in the city or in the country. The tool handles were the work of wood turners; wheelwrights made the light plows used by the peasants, but also the handles of spades and pickaxes, the winnowing scoops and all kinds of farming implements. Casks or, especially, small kegs were used to transport water and different liquids, notably oil; they were the product of the coopers. The weaving looms, so numerous in Fez and the surrounding region, were set up on the premises by specialized workmen; others made the leather buckets used by the dyers and tanners; still others adjusted the spinning wheels indispensable to the weavers. Ropemakers braided hemp ropes which served to secure the loads on the backs of pack animals, or that were used to draw water from the wells, or even made the twine necessary to many trades.

Other workmen were specialists in domestic apparatus: these were the cabinetmakers who made low, round tables, a few sets of shelves, and especially the chests where the trousseaux of the young engaged girls were kept and which, in most houses, took the place of wardrobes, of strong boxes, and of bookcases, for, as has been seen, furniture was rather sparse in the residences of Fez. There were also mat makers to weave the mats which covered the floor of the prayer rooms, and of many poor homes; lantern makers, since there was no public lighting and, on moonless nights, it was indispensable to light one's own way in the narrow dark little streets. Basket makers wove flat baskets and hampers of all sizes in which vegetables, fruit, poultry, even loads of wheat or barley, were transported. Humble artisans made little brooms of dwarf palm. Near the river, coppersmiths made the deep copper pans in which part of the cooking was done.

Certain corporations worked especially for the tribes of

the surrounding countryside, about thirty miles around. This was the case of the wheelwrights, mentioned earlier, who provided the farmers of the neighboring territory with farming implements; it was the same for sieve makers and ropemakers. The farriers, almost always established in the immediate vicinity of the city gates, shod the mules and horses of their fellow citizens, but, to an even greater extent, the riding horses and pack animals of the country people who had come to the market. The armorers worked for the sovereign's army, but also and perhaps primarily, for the military tribes established all around Fez. They had to be ready to send contingents at the first call, with their mounts and their weapons: swords, lances, battle-axes, longbows, crossbows, and bucklers. The same work-men also knew how to make simple or damascened bits and stirrups. The cloaks of coarse wool were chiefly destined for the country people of the neighborhood: the material was rough but of close weave and, consequently, warm and almost waterproof. Combs for animals and also for human beings were made of horn by a corporation whose name is still borne by one of the city streets. And lastly, tapers and candles were also the work of the artisans of Fez and found a considerable clientele among the country people of the neighborhood; they were made of yellow wax, with a heavy hemp wick, and, when tapers to be burned before a saint's tomb were concerned, they were decorated with little thongs of painted parchment. Manifestly the industry of Fez disposed of a large part of its products among the tribes installed around the city.

Fez also had the trade of several Moroccan cities, especially the nearest ones, such as Taza to the east and Meknes to the west, but more distant ones too, such as Salé (Rabat was still only a miserable little huddle of buildings), and even Marrakech. In fact, the luxury products of Fez industry were famous throughout all middle class Morocco, and the other cities bought in Fez fabrics, footwear, headgear, or sent to Fez for workers like the mosaists, makers of stuccowork friezes or painters. Many dwellings in all the cities of Morocco were decorated by artisans from Fez, who thus absented themselves for weeks, sometimes for months, in order to work outside Fez.

And lastly, the industry of Fez maintained a commerce of longer range. It does not seem that its products were sold in Europe, but they found purchasers in several countries of North Africa and even of East Africa, and also in black Africa. It appears probable that the commerce of Fez with countries situated to the east was closely linked with the pilgrimage to Mecca. It was a question of an onerous journey that many undertook carrying with them merchandise from Fez, which they sold little by little along their way, bringing back, in exchange, other merchandise from the east, which they disposed of on the return trip. Expensive clothing and jewels, which will be mentioned again further along, furnished the essential part of the merchandise sold in this way in central Maghreb, now called Algeria, in Ifriqiya, the Tunisia of today, in Tripolitania, in Egypt, and probably as far as in the holy cities. In connection with black Africa, the relations were more strictly commercial. For a long time, at least since the Almoravide domination, Fez had organized, through the intermediary of caravans leaving Tafilalet, trade with the cities of the Niger bend, Gao and Timbuctoo, which bought certain luxury articles from local industry. Thus it can be said that the weavers, the tanners, and the whole body of related trade corporations, the dyers, the spinners, the shoemakers, etc., worked to a certain extent for export into distant countries.

The Jewish artisans had their part in all this: certain trades were traditionally their portion, notably those of which metal was the essential raw material, probably for magic reasons, the Moslem workmen being loath to manipulate certain metals. A large proportion of Jewish workers could therefore be found among the lantern makers and the damasceners, and it may be said that they had the monopoly for manufacturing the combs for carding wool, and especially for jewelry; they were therefore the ones who worked gold and silver to make arm bracelets and ankle bracelets, earrings, necklaces, breastplates, and rings, often with a consummate art.

All these workers, except the women who worked at home, were organized into trade guilds. In the present state of documentation, it is not possible to fix precisely the origin of the corporations of Fez—were they borrowed directly from the Arabian east or were they of Andalusian origin? Perhaps it would be possible to answer these questions if it were known when the corporation system was established in Fez. But the authors who touch upon this city remain silent on this point and it can only be affirmed that in the Middle Ages the trade corporations did exist, without its being possible to say since what date or under what influence.

These groupings were, in general, technical groupings, that is to say, they brought together workmen employed in the same trade, whatever might be the geographical locality of their workshops. However, if what was happening among the tanners is taken into account, it must be admitted that certain corporations presented a geographical character, since the four tanneries of Fez constituted three corporative groups, one of these tanneries, much less important than the others, being attached to one of the three other corporations. It may therefore be said that, in general and admitting a few exceptions, the corporations brought together workmen of a same technique. All workmen were part of the corporation, even the youngest apprentices, but the latter were content with benefiting from the advantages procured by the group, without participating in its management. There existed, in fact, within the corporations a hierarchy of three degrees: the classifications of employers, workmen, and apprentices. This hierarchy, more clearly marked in the corporations having many members than in the others, had no rigidly fixed character. In order to become a workman, the apprentice had at least to have attained the age of puberty and to know how to ply his trade correctly, but he was not obliged to pass an examination in order to prove it; this was an affair arranged between his employer, himself, and sometimes his family. In the same way, a workman could become an employer at will: it sufficed for him to have at his disposition the little capital necessary to set up his establishment, and to find an appropriate site, as well as a clientele. In actual fact, it appears that the situation of the different categories of workers was highly stable and that passage from one to the other was by way of seniority, or through chance openings created by illness or death. The difference between workmen and apprentices was great at least at the outset: the one was a child, the other a man; one knew his trade, the other was beginning to learn it; one earned his living, the other had the right only to small rewards for the little services that he could render; then, little by little, the differences lessened, the apprentice fathomed the secrets of the trade, the gifts took on importance and were transformed into wages, up to the moment when, knowing the essentials of his task and receiving a fixed stipend, the apprentice became a workman. However, at any given moment, the workman and the apprentice had this in common—they did not participate directly in the life of the corporation, a privilege reserved for the employers. Granted this difference, employers and workers led much the same existence. Certainly the employer was concerned with the sale of the finished products, with the commercial aspect of the enterprise, though he sometimes confided this task to an experienced worker, but as far as the technique itself was concerned, the workman had the same knowledge as his employer and at times surpassed him in manual skill. As for resources, save in a few exceptional cases of owners of weaving establishments, these did not differ very much in either case, for industry in Fez was not very remunerative, at least when products for current consumption were concerned, and if the owner, in a period of high prices, made a few small profits, he also bore the expenses of the enterprise; taking everything into account, his standard of living was not much higher, if indeed it was higher at all. But the owner was an active member of his corporation; he participated in the general meetings, when any were held, and in the naming of the dignitaries of the corporation, when this was required.

It does not seem that these nominations obeyed fixed rules. These dignitaries, that is to say, the head of the corporation, his "confidential agent," *amin* as he was called in Arabic, the deputy of the *amin* and the few proprietors, in a restricted but not strictly fixed number, who constituted the corporation council, were not named for a set period: age, death, or some special circumstance alone put an end to their period of service. Moreover they were not elected, properly speaking, by the corporation, but recommended by it for appointment by the *muhtasib*, exactly as the district heads were recommended by the notables for appointment by the governor. This recommendation did not take the form of an election in the modern sense of the word; it was the result of one or several meetings during which discussion took place at greater or less length and with more or less passion, until it ended finally in unanimous agreement on the name or names to be proposed to the authorities.

The role of the corporation is not always easy to define with precision. In any case, it would be erroneous to compare it with that of our modern trade-unions; it was much more restricted. The guild had a role of mutual aid: when one of its members, owner, workman, or apprentice, was struck down by illness or death, the corporation brought to him or to his family material and moral support; it did not possess for this purpose specific resources, but made an appeal, never in vain it seems, to the generosity of its members who gave their time and their money, according to their means. In addition, in case of litigation, within the corporation itself or with purveyors or customers, the dignitaries of the corporation brought to the *muhtasib* the assistance of their technical experience and their wisdom: they constituted the group, limited in general, of experts on whom the *muhtasib* called for enlightenment. Finally, the dignitaries of the corporation played the role of executive agents of the central power when it was a question of applying to each corporation measures of a general nature. For example, when the government imposed upon one corporation or another an obligation to execute works of general interest, the distribution of tasks was effected within the group, in the same way as the assessments of extraordinary taxes; it was customary, for example, for the different groups of the city to offer gifts to the sovereign on the occasion of the great festivals, or of a marriage, or a victory; the share of each one was fixed by the corporation council. The dignitaries had also to organize the corporative festivals: each corporation, or at least the more important ones, was placed under the patronage of a saint. This was sometimes a poor workman who had acquired, God knows when and how, a reputation for saintliness; such was the case of the potters' patron saint, Sidi Mimun the Potter, whose tomb was near the workshops where he had spent his life, and about whom nothing was known any more except a few edifying legends. In other cases, it was a famous scholar who, at some moment in his life and for obscure reasons, had become interested in a certain guild: the patron saint of the shoemakers was Sidi Muhammad Ibn'Abbad, who had never held a shoemaker's knife in his life, but had handled a pen with skill. All these saints, brilliant or humble, were honored once a year on a fixed date by their protégés: this was a day for prayers, but also for revelry, at times even a day of professional activity, as in the case of Sidi'Abi Bu Ghalib, patron saint of the barbers, in whose honor these worthy men arranged in his mausoleum a session of circumcision gratis. Besides, all the corporations participated in the festivals organized in honor of the patron saint of the city. It is not certain that in the fourteenth century the festivals in honor of Mawlay Idris had assumed as much solemnity as they had later on; it was not until the fifteenth century that the worship of this saint was to take on the amplitude characteristic of it since. It is probable however that his memory was already honored, and in any case, there was no lack of collective celebrations, religious or secular, of which the artisans had their share.

It is evident that the role of the guilds was far more social than technical. Excluding the expert appraisals that the *muhtasib* required of them, the guilds were much more occupied with charitable duties or handling of complaints than with professional activities. They did not concern themselves, it seems, with organizing, and even less with improving, their own activities. These activities had existed for centuries; they allowed life to proceed without too much difficulty; no one, apparently, thought of re-examining them. As they were not threatened from the outside, since no external influence affected the life of Fez, no one had the idea that there might be, in this respect, any matter for thought, and still less for action.

According to their techniques, the different corporations carried on their activities on varied premises. Certain ones needed a relatively large space and special installations: the tanners could not get along without a whole set of vats and basins for macerating and rinsing the skins after the different operations; the potters needed ovens, sites for storing their reserve stocks of fuel, and, especially, spacious drying areas where they exposed objects to the sunlight before firing; the oil mills also needed room. But most of the artisans of the city could manage with quarters that were interchangeable, or nearly so. Sometimes these were workshops, often on the ground floor of a warehouse, whose upper floors served some other purpose, or else ateliers expressly constructed, spacious enough to shelter several weaver's looms, or again simple shops, similar in all respects to those of the merchants; they all faced on the street, to which they were largely open; sometimes their floor was at the same level as the street, sometimes it was raised above it as much as a yard at most. Thus a large part of the work in Fez was done under everybody's eyes, and that contributed to the intimacy of the artisans and the city, which appears as a characteristic of the handicraft industries of Fez.

The work rhythm varied according to the seasons and the religious festivals. In winter, the day was shorter, for work was done only by natural light; in summer, it was longer. They began after the morning prayer and meal, when it was full daylight; there was a recess for the noon prayer, followed by light refreshments taken on the spot, and they stopped with the midafternoon prayer, unless there was urgent work to be done, in which case the day ended only with the sunset prayer. They were idle in general all of Friday morning, so that the workers could accomplish the ritual ablutions before the solemn noon prayer. On the occasion of religious festivals, work ceased for two or three days on the average, without any general rule's fixing the duration of the period of idleness; extraordinary festivities, such as the feasts of a patron saint, or the celebration of a great event, for example the return of the sovereign after a victorious military expedition, again interrupted all professional activities for one or two days. Finally, throughout the month of Ramadan, the month of fasting, activity was slowed down: work rarely began until late in the morning and stopped in time for each one to be at home again for the breaking of the fast, at the hour of sundown. It may be said that the industrial activity of Fez received its rhythm from the call of the muezzin atop the minarets, and from the evolution of the liturgical calendar. This activity proceeded according to a moderate rhythm except when, for one reason or another, the economic needs of the city increased suddenly and workmen had to speed up at their tasks. But, as far as we are able to find out, these spurts of economic fever were neither frequent nor sizable.

In general, the stock of tools used by these industries was not complicated. Naturally the only, or almost only, motive force employed was human energy. The millers alone employed a natural force, water running down a slope to make their millstones turn, and, in the oil mills, an animal was utilized for the operation of other millstones. All the others counted only on their strength and their skill. As has been said earlier, the tools were entirely of local manufacture. They were relatively complicated when weaving looms were concerned, especially those which served for making luxury materials; this was however an exception. A few cutting instruments, hammers, pincers, thread, needles, a few pieces of bamboo, some pottery shards, twine; this was all the artisans of Fez needed for the exercise of their skill. It is easy then to understand why, in the majority of cases, the workman who wanted to set up his own business did not need a large outlay of capital: his stock of tools did not cost him much.

Almost all the raw materials came from the region, not more than thirty miles around on the average, and sometimes from the city itself: this was the case with the pigeon droppings used by the tanners for certain baths in which they macerated the skins. They had to do scarcely more than stoop to gather this material, for pigeons nested in great numbers in all the buildings of Fez. Precious metals alone came from a distance; gold especially was imported from the Sudan, but it should be added immediately that old jewels were frequently sold locally, and were made over into others: the quantity of new gold imported each year must have been quite small. The tanners also imported from Tafilalet a tanning product, the gall of the tamarisk, which they called by its Berber name of *takawt*. Cedarwood came from the forests of the Middle Atlas, olivewood from the northern regions; the country surrounding Fez was rich in flocks, foodstuffs, and olives; limestone and building stone, sand, and clay abounded in the immediate neighborhood; silkworms were reared, for mulberry trees grew in abundance; the small amount of cotton and flax necessary to the industry of the city was cultivated. The mineral products used by the crockery makers or the dyers also came from the region. The industry of Fez did not depend, therefore, on supplies brought in from a distance, that is to say costly and uncertain, except in so far as *takawt* was concerned. This had to be obtained two hundred fifty miles from the city and arrived with difficulty in winter, when the mountain passes were blocked by snow; but, save in the case of severe cold, the passes were not closed all winter long and the tanners took their precautions. Even in the case of disturbances, rare in the period under consideration, the industry of Fez could be maintained without great difficulty: this was clearly seen in the fifteenth century, when Morocco was practically cut in two; even deprived of regular communications with the region of Marrakech, industry in Fez pursued its activity as if nothing had happened. The whole of Morocco would have to be ablaze, as was to be the case during all the first half of the seventeenth century, for the industrial activity of Fez to suffer seriously from the political situation.

Techniques were as simple as tools and raw materials: they were based entirely on the dexterity of the workers, that is to say, on a long training which began in their earliest years, and on the heed that they paid to their work.

The maintenance and dismantling of the tools posed no problems, the diverse operations to be carried out had been known for centuries and did not undergo any changes. Perhaps in certain families little "manufacturing secrets" were transmitted from father to son, but these were quite small secrets, and, even if some one of them disappeared, as a consequence of a sudden death, the economy of the trade was not altered by this fact.

In general, the industrial enterprises were small in extent. The weaving industry, by far the most prosperous, was perhaps an exception to the rule; certain indications permit the inference that a few owners of large weaving establishments possessed some twoscore or more looms and employed up to fifty workmen, but such cases were rare. In general, an employer had around him only five or six workers or apprentices and it often happened, in the shops of shoemakers and many others, that the owner worked alone with an apprentice who was his son.

Under these conditions man power could only be stable. In the history of Fez during the fourteenth century there is no visible trace of serious industrial crises, of periods of idleness followed by feverish activity. This resulted from the fact that the rhythm of production was constant; at the most it was subject to fluctuations of restricted amplitude caused by the variations of the climate. When the agricultural year was favorable, the peasants of the surrounding country had something to sell and they increased their buying in the city; when on the contrary too severe a drouth or an overabundant rainfall had jeopardized the crops, the peasants put off their purchases until better times. It does not seem that the equilibrium was ever seriously threatened in the middle of the fourteenth century. It appears, in addition, that the population was fairly stable and that at no time was there an afflux of starving peasants toward the cities. Overall, with the exception of a transient body of day laborers, and the suburban residents, who must not have been numerous, the majority of the workmen were recruited on the spot, often from father to son or uncle to nephew. If a more abundant documentation were available, it would probably be possible to note some circumstantial variations, but they were never considerable: in the contrary case, some indication would be found in the chronicles which do not fail to mention extraordinary events.

Since precise details are lacking, it is possible to form only a general idea of the circumstances of the workmen. They did not have an easy life, and the employers, except in the case of a few enterprising individuals, did not grow rich. The names of people of high rank are an indication that rarely misleads—these names are generally given in full and end, for individuals of nearby rural origin, with the name of their tribe, and for old city dwellers, with the name of their family, which is often a nickname or the name of a trade. Among those who attained a prominent position and whose complete names are known to us, practically no name of a trade is found. Granted that some may have succeeded in discarding a patronymic which recalled a humble origin, the case must not have been frequent in this city where everyone was acquainted, and the indication is valid from the over-all point of view. Workers, like employers, earned only enough to live on and some had a great deal of difficulty, if they had a numerous family to support. Nevertheless, aside from exceptional cases, they did not fall into want and, moreover, they had the feeling of being a part of the city, of counting for something there in the eyes of all. Indeed, if the em-

ployer and the workman earned but little, they were recognized and enjoyed the esteem of the other inhabitants.
Not all of them equally, however, for there existed a moral
hierarchy of the trades. The weavers, the tanners, the leath-
erworkers, the dyers, who belonged to the guilds having
the most members, were justly considered to be the essential elements of the city's activity. The skilled workmen, in contact with the élite of the city through the force
of circumstances, and renowned for their taste and ability,
derived from all this a deserved importance. Certain trades,
on the contrary, were reputed to be dirty and moreover
were scarcely ever exercised by any save strangers in the
city; such were the workers in the oil mills. And lastly
some, especially those where metal was manipulated, were
deemed dubious: those who practiced them might have
knowledge of magic and use it. They were feared and
scorned at the same time and that is why they were frequently left to the Jewish artisans.

However, in the over-all picture, the artisans held a
place, an honorable one, in the moral hierarchy of the city
because they were numerous, because they participated
actively in the life of the body social, and because they
gave proof in general of a high degree of professional integrity. If by chance one of them failed in this respect,
everyone rose in protest against him, beginning with his
peers, for the dishonor he incurred might affect them.
Besides, these breaches in the honor of the trade were
harshly penalized by the *muhtasib*. There existed for many
of the guilds a pillory where defective articles were exposed with the name of the inferior worker; thus the whole
city quickly knew that so-and-so was a dishonest artisan
and he had no other expedient but to leave the city. Certain articles, such as foodstuffs, could not be put on the

pillory. Then the *muhtasib* condemned the delinquent to the "degrading promenade": if a butcher had sold spoiled meat, the *muhtasib* had it cut in pieces; a sort of necklace was made of it and hung around the neck of the condemned man, and he was obliged to walk through the whole city, under the escort of the agents of the *muhtasib*, all the while confessing his crime aloud. The middle class of Fez was also grateful to the artisans for being temperate people; they rarely set off political disturbances; not until the end of the nineteenth century, at the beginning of the reign of Mawlay al-Hasan, is there certainty of a revolt organized by the tanners, and chroniclers speak of it as a scandalous and quite unusual event. Admittedly the artisans of Fez participated more than once in political upheavals, in rebellions against the established power, but in that case they only joined mass movements of which they were rarely the instigators, and such was not the case in the fourteenth century. In short, this important body of workers gives the impression of an honest and peaceful group, perfectly integrated into the city as a whole.

The manufacture of articles is not the whole story; they must be sold, and this is the occasion for examining the commercial activity of the city. As a general rule, sale and purchase were entirely free, but in actual fact the industrial production of Fez was disposed of chiefly through the procedure of auction sales. The artisans of Fez had an unquestioned right to sell directly to private individuals or to merchants and they did so from time to time, but this procedure did not assure them a regular and constant market; consequently in general they preferred to sell at auction. At regular intervals—every day for babouches, fabrics, raw wool, and for all raw materials and products for current consumption, once or twice a week for the other things—an auction took place, always held on the same spot; most often this was the courtyard of a warehouse, but sometimes it was the street or the square where the merchants, the principal buyers, had their shops. It was rare for an auction to last more than two hours, and it was generally held after the midafternoon prayer. The play, for this was truly a comedy in which each played his part, proceeded among three categories of persons: the sellers and the buyers, to be sure, and the auctioneers who put them in touch with one another, and whom we shall call criers for the convenience of the account. The criers formed as many corporations as there were public auctions; their number in each one varied naturally according to the importance of the product to be sold: criers of textiles and leather goods were clearly more numerous than the others. They were called in Arabic the "displayers" (*dellala*), for their principal role consisted of exhibiting and enhancing the value of the articles entrusted to them in order to obtain the best price for them; this was to their interest, since they were paid in proportion to the price obtained.

Sellers arrived at the accustomed hour and chose their crier; most of the time they had a regular crier, whom they had the habit of using and in whom they had confidence. The buyers were there also; they took their places according to the premises so as to leave free space where the criers could circulate without too much difficulty. However, as the auction site was usually small, the unbiased observer had an impression of a disorderly swarming mass which did not withstand careful scrutiny. Products to be sold were divided into sale units which varied from one auction to another; for example, footwear was sold by three, six, or twelve pairs, raw skins, by six or twelve, except for oxhides which were sold singly, and so forth. The criers passed in front of the purchasers, displaying the articles, and announcing in a loud voice the asking price. When a buyer made himself known by a simple gesture, the crier went to find the seller to ascertain whether he consented to the sale, remitted the merchandise to the buyer, and put up another lot. The sale was generally made for cash and, in this case, the buyer benefitted by a good will reduction in price, analogous to the "discount" of our day, which was traditional and not subject to discussion. The purchaser remitted to the crier the agreed price, plus the customary commission, and the crier paid the seller the sum to which he was entitled, less his commission. It sometimes happened that the buyer asked for an extension of time for payment; if he obtained it, the good will reduction no longer had any justification. This market naturally experienced fluctuations; prices went up when the demand was strong, that is to say a few days before the great festivals, or at the end of the agricultural season, when the peasants, after selling their harvest, had the means to make purchases beyond what was strictly necessary. Prices went down immediately after the festivals, for a good part of the population had spent a great deal of money in order to celebrate properly, and had to limit themselves for a time to strictly necessary purchases; they went down again at the end of the spring, when the peasants had exhausted their yearly reserves and were waiting for the proceeds of the harvest before buying. More irregular and more widespread phenomena also interfered with the rhythm of the auction sales. Good or bad agricultural years had their repercussions; also political events, military campaigns, internal crises, etc. It is evident that in this system the sellers, that is to say the artisans, who almost never had substantial reserves, were in an unfavorable position, for they had to sell, come what may. On the contrary, the buyers, who were sometimes important and extremely rich merchants, had time to wait, and were almost always able to buy at the time when prices were favorable to them. However, many small merchants did not have considerable floating capital and were obliged to buy almost from day to day. They may be said to constitute the regulating element of the market. Naturally, several corporations avoided the auction system, and were subject to the system of sale by private contract. This was the case for all the corporations which worked in the construction industry; there, there was a direct agreement between the consumer and the producer.

Products sold at auction were bought by a few individuals, but rarely so, each lot being generally too large for family use. In a larger number of cases, they were bought directly by processors when a semifinished product was concerned, one which still had to undergo some modifications before reaching the consumer, or in the case of a raw material. Thus skeins of raw wool or silk were bought directly by the weavers, raw skins by the tanners, tanned skins by the shoemakers, the makers of leather bags, or others. However, the majority of the purchases were made by merchants, wholesalers or retailers who were in comfortable circumstances.

Not a great deal is known about the wholesalers of the Marinide epoch, except that they existed; a few beautiful residences that certain of them had built, and which still stand, prove that they made rather large profits, but no details of their activity are available. Certain indications, however, permit the inference that they undertook two types of business, domestic and foreign. In proportion to the capital at their disposal they, almost alone, were capable of building up substantial stocks of the products of local industry that they then resold, day by day, to the retailers. In addition, they were in control of the foreign trade of Fez. They were the ones who bought from European merchants established at Melilla, Badis, and Ceuta articles of value, notably fabrics, which found purchasers among the wealthy families of the principal cities, Fez in particular, and at the court. It was they also who financed the "commerce of the pilgrimage," that is to say, the sale of products of local industry that some carried into the countries situated to the east of Morocco, on the occasion of the annual caravan of the pilgrimage. Lastly, they are the ones who, thanks to agents established at Tafilalet and perhaps in certain cities of the Niger bend, organized the caravans which transported into the Sudan fabrics and leathers from Fez, and brought back gold dust, ostrich plumes, and also slaves. This foreign commerce was doubtless not considerable as to tonnage, but, in proportion to the value of the products exported, to their small quantity itself, and to the risks run, which could not fail to be liberally estimated, it was certainly lucrative and, in addition, included that portion of uncertainty and gambling that the great merchants of Fez liked. The profits were certainly reinvested in new enterprises for one part, and, for another, in the acquisition of real estate or of building sites, upon which the merchants had beautiful residences erected. Thus the industry of the city profited directly from the sale of the exported products and indirectly from the use that the merchants made of their gains. But it does not appear that the merchants invested the funds at their disposition in new industrial ventures, judging probably that the nearly constant sale of the products of Fez did not justify a more ample development.

The retailers were of two kinds: those who sold relatively precious articles, fabrics, footwear, jewels, spices, and who were installed in the central market, the *Qisariya,* and those who sold in various quarters of the city products for daily consumption, notably foodstuffs, eggs, butter, oil, soap, fruit, etc. The first were people in comfortable circumstances because the products that they handled were relatively expensive, their clientele was fairly rich, and in consequence their margin of profit was sizable. They occupied different little streets of the *Qisariya;* thus there was the market for woolen cloth, for silk materials, for jewels, for candles, for spices, and for footwear. All the shops of the same specialty were located side by side. This grouping of merchants by specialty is in every way comparable to that which existed in Europe in the Middle Ages, with this exception: there does not appear to have existed in Europe any equivalent of the *Qisariya*, a site filled entirely with shops, where no one lived, and which was completely closed down at nightfall, with only a few night watchmen charged with preventing fires and thefts. The merchants of the *Qisariya* formed a part, at least, of what might be called the average middle class of the city.

The other retailers were in a less favorable situation: the nature of their products and the anomalous character of their clientele did not permit them to make large profits. In addition, they could count only on the clientele of their quarter, for, if peasants and transient travelers frequented the *Qisariya*, they did not visit the retailers of the various quarters, save sometimes those who were installed near the principal gates of the city. The retailers therefore formed, for the most part, a class of poor merchants whose standard of living was quite close to that of the artisans. Often obliged to buy merchandise on credit, they depended closely on the wholesalers, who alone were in a position to grant delayed payments.

Such was, in general outline, the economic life of Fez in the fourteenth century, at least as far as it is possible for us to know it. It is immediately evident that it had a rather limited character. Fez was not one of those great mercantile cities which played an important role in the commercial and industrial activity of the ancient world, such as Cairo and Alexandria, Baghdad and Basra, Aleppo and even Tunis, or, outside the Moslem world, such as Constantinople, Smyrna, and several large Italian cities, not to mention the trade centers of non-Mediterranean Europe. This relatively modest activity was due primarily to the geographical position of the city. In the fourteenth century, Morocco was in a remote corner of the old world, apart from the great commercial routes of the Mediterranean. It must not be forgotten that, in that period, the Atlantic was an empty ocean—only at the end of the fifteenth century would the Portuguese begin to give it life by opening the route of the Cape of Good Hope, after having founded numerous commercial settlements on the Atlantic coast of Africa, and not until the beginning of the sixteenth century was traffic with America to receive its impetus. In the scheme of maritime links Morocco was therefore far out of center; it was scarcely less so in the scheme of connections with black Africa by way of the Sahara. On this point, in fact, it suffered from strong competition on the part of Tlemcen, which through the oases of Zuzfana and Twat, was no further distant than Fez from the Nigerian Sudan; moreover the ports which served Tlemcen—Hunayn, Rashgun, at the mouth of the Tafna, and Oran—were more easily accessible to Italian ships, the most active at this time in the western Mediterranean, than were the ports of Fez. Finally, the Iberian Peninsula, with which Fez was in a good geographic position to maintain commercial ties, was practically closed to Moslem commerce because of the Christian Reconquest, during whose course Moroccans and Castilians often clashed, weapons in hand. The commerce of Fez and the outlets open to its industry had therefore a marked local character.

But if this economic activity was limited for the reasons just mentioned, it was carried on in the fourteenth century in a calm and unified Morocco, and in the heart of a region favorable to agriculture, and relatively prosperous. Under these conditions, the economic activity of the city was far from being negligible, as has been seen, and showed a quality of marked stability that only grave Moroccan crises could disturb; but such was not the case in the fourteenth century, since the Marinide power was firmly rooted and order reigned. The skill of the artisans and the wisdom, at the same time as the enterprising spirit, of the merchants, compensated to a certain degree for the geographical position of Fez and the restricted scope which resulted from it.

VI

INTELLECTUAL LIFE

It MAY BE INFERRED, although precise information on the subject is not available, that Fez was from the outset a center of Moslem education and Arabic culture. In fact, this city was isolated at the western extremity of the Islamic world; it did not have, in reasonable proximity, any center of Moslem education where it might send its sons who were desirous of receiving instruction. Tlemcen and Tangier were scarcely better endowed; Spain was far away and probably hostile or at least suspicious of the Idrissides. The nascent city was thus thrown back upon its own resources; it behooved it to maintain through its own means a seat of Moslem learning. There were perhaps a few scholars in the entourage of the two Idrises; it is probable also that, among the Córdoban and Kairwanian emigrants who came to settle in Fez at the beginning of the ninth century, there were some erudite men. At the end of the tenth century, when the Ommayyads of Spain established a sort of protectorate over northern Morocco, Fez included, it is likely that the Andalusian influence was exerted in the domain of the intellect as it was in matters of technique. But, until the advent of the Almoravides, the intellectual center thus constituted certainly remained modest and was scarcely heard of.

Did these Saharan and Berber conquerors, refined and guided by Andalusian influence, give a strong impetus to the intellectual life of Fez? The attention they brought to bear on the enlarging and decorating of the Mosque of the Kairwanians is evidence of their religious preoccupations. But on the other hand, when the promoter of the Almohade movement, Ibn Tumart, decided to go "questing for knowledge," according to the picturesque Arabic expression, it was not to Fez that he betook himself at the beginning of the twelfth century, but to Córdoba first and afterwards to the Orient. In this era, Idris's city does not appear to have offered him the intellectual broadening that he desired. When, fifteen years later, he returned from the Orient, he sought out the savants of Fez, but neither more nor less so than those of Tlemcen or elsewhere. It is thus permissible to say that the intellectual development of Fez was slow; during the whole Almoravide and Almohade periods, Marrakech was the center of Morocco, for intellectual as well as political life; it was to Marrakech that the philosophers Ibn Tufayl and Averrhoes repaired when they came from Spain to Morocco. In the domain of the intellect, as in the others, the Marinides were responsible for a slow, but durable and profound, expansion. It was at their instigation that Fez became and remained the intellectual capital of Morocco and of the whole western half of Maghreb.

As is often the case, intellectual life in Fez developed around a center of learning which took on important proportions in the period under consideration. This center of learning grew slowly and assumed the customary form of Moslem centers of learning in the Middle Ages, that is to say, it was composed of what we might call elementary schools, Koranic schools, and several mosques or colleges, properly so called, where a more advanced instruction was given.

We have no specific information concerning the Koranic schools in the Marinide epoch; assuredly they resembled all the Koranic schools of the entire Moslem world. Boys were sent there from the age of five or six years. Under the ferule of a single schoolmaster, who directed the studies of all the children gathered around him, whatever might be their age and the level of their attainments, they learned to read and write the text of the Koran and endeavored to commit it to memory. At the same time, by dint of circumstances, they were initiated little by little into Arabic grammar and language, although that was not the direct objective of the instruction, this objective being primarily the mnemotechnic knowledge of the sacred text. The classroom was sometimes contiguous to a mosque and was always put at the disposition of the schoolmaster and the students, without charge, by the service of religious properties. The schoolmaster was a poor man, who had as his capital only the memorization of the Koran, and received every week from each of his pupils a slight remuneration, plus gifts in cash or in kind, on the occasion of the great Moslem festivals, or the little private festivities at school, notably on the day when one of the pupils had committed to memory the entire text of the Koran. Each pupil had at his disposal a small wooden plank, a goose quill, and a little inkstand, and wrote on his board the text of the daily lesson. Once this text was thoroughly learned, in principle for life, the pupil washed off his board, and wrote a new text from the schoolmaster's dictation. The children, who lived in the vicinity of the school arrived early, after the meal at the beginning of the morning, squatted on the mats with which the floor was covered and remained thus until around noon, when they returned home for their meal. They came back immediately afterwards, and resumed studying until the midafternoon prayer, which marked the end of their workday. These two daily sessions were devoted to writing and learning by heart the fragment which had to be memorized in the space of one or two days—a very brief selection, only a few lines, for the beginners, as soon as they learned how to trace Arabic characters, a much longer fragment for the students accustomed to this work. Except in the case where two pupils began their studies at the same time and gave proof of the same intellectual aptitudes, the texts assigned were, in actual fact, different. They were learned aloud, according to a psalmody into which the children were initiated from the beginning. From each Koranic school arouse therefore a discordant concert of childish voices, reciting in earsplitting tones varied passages from the Koran. The uninitiated auditor experienced, upon hearing this, an impression of cacophony and disorder. The master himself was attuned to it and when one of his pupils made a mistake, he seized from beside him a slender rod, more or less long, according to whether the pupil was seated near him or far away, and without stirring from his place, gave one or more taps of the rod on the head or the shoulders of the offending child. In case of serious misbehavior, laziness or breach of discipline, the culprit was vigorously seized by some older students; his feet were enclosed in a wooden framework made for this purpose and the schoolmaster lashed the soles of them with as many blows of the rod as the misconduct merited.

A strange pedagogy, so contrary to our modern principles of education! It cannot be denied however that it had, and still preserves in our day, a certain efficacy. It could not be maintained that all the children who passed through the Koranic school learned the Koran by heart;

at least they all learned long fragments of it which remained with them for the rest of their days, and they were trained, for their whole lives, in Moslem good manners, because the Koran master was not solely a technician, charged with inculcating certain knowledge in his pupils; he was also an educator who taught them how a good Moslem ought to conduct himself in daily life. It is nonetheless true that, on the intellectual plane, this teaching had as its essential merit the development of the memory, but scarcely went beyond that, since instruction in the grammar and the language had no systematic character and was given only at random according to the Koranic texts, difficult texts even for the best informed.

Most children, at least the sons of poor families, did not go beyond the level of the Koranic school, and many of them left it before having learned the whole Koran by heart. Those who attained this goal, toward the age of thirteen or fourteen years, and had the resources or found a means for pursuing their studies, undertook an instruction that might be called intermediate, but whose general organization was vague. In fact, anyone could teach, on condition of obtaining authorization from the cadi, who consulted in this matter the principal scholars of Fez. One who had received such authorization let it be known in the city that he was going to offer a course on such and such a subject, and generally in a mosque or a religious edifice, where he taught outside the hours for prayers. He took for his subject grammar and the elements of law or theology, and his success depended on his patrons, and also on his qualifications and his competence. It was not a question, therefore, of instruction organized by the state, but only controlled by the state and of unequal value. Nevertheless, it may be inferred that in Fez only relatively competent men undertook such a task, the others would not have had any pupils. Their pupils knew the Koran by heart, were able to read, write, and chant, and possessed some practical rudiments of Arabic lexicography and grammar. The master's task was to maintain them in their knowledge of the Koran and to inculcate in them some theoretical elements of Arabic grammar and Moslem law. As in the Koranic schools, there was no fixed program, or specified time for the duration of studies. When the pupil, his father, and his teacher or teachers considered that he was sufficiently instructed, he proceeded into what might be termed higher education.

It is evident that the Marinides gave substantial support to the development of higher education in Fez; they may be considered the true creators of the "University of Fez." The institution of numerous establishments of learning, the *madrasas,* is evidence in the proof. What were their incentives for such a course of action? They certainly desired to give their capital new luster and to make it the principal intellectual city of their kingdom, as it was the principal political city and the principal economic city. Their religious zeal was doubtless an element in it also: contrary to the Almoravides and the Almohades, they had not seized power in the name of a religious ideal; perhaps they felt this was a hiatus which might be prejudicial to them and they desired to give themselves a prestige which they lacked. But it should be noted also that the institutions they created were as much student lodgings as schools. Everything transpired therefore as if they had sought to control the intellectual and religious training of the most gifted young men of the Moroccan countryside. This was the period which saw the development in Morocco of a popular mystical current which seems to have acquired a certain strength from the beginning of the thirteenth century. On the doctrinal plane this movement presented rather serious risks of heresy; on the political plane it ran the risk of turning to anarchy, for the influence of the rural mystics tended to overstep the boundaries of pure religion and become active in the domain of politics also. The Marinides appear to have endeavored to curb these centrifugal tendencies by summoning to Fez those who must have constituted the rural élite, and by subjecting them to the rules of a strict orthodoxy at the same time as a certain political discipline. In any case, the presence in Fez of a fairly large number—several hundred in the middle of the fourteenth century—of young men coming from the principal regions of Morocco was a new phenomenon and one which assumed great importance. It conferred upon Fez a sort of intellectual sovereignty over the whole country which the city had scarcely enjoyed up to that time. This was certainly not the first time that young men, strangers to the city, had come there to receive instruction, but up to that time they had necessarily been only in small numbers, since they encountered many difficulties in finding lodging. The creation of institutions set up expressly to receive them doubtless led them to come in much greater numbers and augmented considerably the lustre of the teachers of Fez.

As has already been indicated, the Marinides do not appear to have conferred upon the Mosque of the Kairwanians a monopoly of instruction. Certainly the most numerous *madrasas* were built around this mosque, which seems to indicate either that it already enjoyed a sort of preeminence, or else that the Marinides wished to bestow this distinction upon it. But the construction of two twin *madrasas* in the vicinity of the Mosque of the Andalusians bears witness to the existence of a flourishing center of learning there also. The erection of another *madrasa* beside the Great Mosque of Fez Jdid proves that the Marinides wanted to make their royal city a third center of learning, and the installation of lecture halls in the vast *madrasa* constructed by Abu 'Inan proves that this sultan had the intention of opening a fourth. What was the motive for this sort of decentralization of teaching? Should it be viewed as the beginning of a specialization of the different schools of Fez? The name of the *Madrasa* of the Seven Fashions of Chanting the Koran seems to indicate it, but this is only a clue from which it would be imprudent to draw peremptory conclusions. It can nevertheless be affirmed that the aggregate of these centers of learning constitutes what might be called the University of Fez.

The teachers formed a sort of corporation of the learned which little by little played an increasingly important role in the intellectual, spiritual, and political life, not only of Fez, but of the whole of Morocco. Unfortunately it is impossible to form an idea of the number of these professors or to learn how they were organized. It is probable that a moral hierarchy, if not an institutional hierarchy, existed among them. In any case, they were recruited by co-optation, since it was on their counsel that the cadi gave authorization for teaching. It is probable that the greater number of them belonged to the local middle class, but it is certain also that they authorized several of their rural pupils to join their ranks, as is attested by the names of several of these masters. An example is Ibn Ajarrum, who died in Fez in 1322. His name is typically Berber and he had been born in the little town of Sefrou, nineteen miles south of Fez, chiefly inhabited by Berbers. He was the author of a treatise on grammar which, in one thousand

verses (from which it takes its name of *Alfiya, alf* signify-
ing one thousand) summarized the essentials of Arabic
grammar and remains in use in our day. It appears evident
also that in spite of professional rivalries which arose
among them, they almost always gave proof of great cohesion: they were conscious of constituting the intellectual
élite of the city and kingdom, and appeared as a body on
important occasions.

It is not certain that they received a fixed salary, but
they enjoyed advantages of lodging and were allotted
gifts in cash or in kind, remitted to them by the government on the occasion of the religious festivals and important events that occurred at the court. Many of them possessed a personal fortune that might be considerable: others
had made wealthy marriages; and finally, others obtained
resources that were far from negligible by giving juridical
consultations. They were, on the whole, in comfortable
circumstances. It may be inferred that almost all, if not
indeed all of them, had pursued their studies in Fez.

The subjects taught were of a religious nature. They
were the exegesis of the Koran and of the prophetic tradition, the theology or science of the unity of God, and
especially law and jurisprudence, which took on greater
and greater importance, and which included ritual. To
these major fields of learning were added grammar, rhet-
oric, prosody, logic, and also elements of mathematics and
astronomy for the calculation of the liturgical calendar and
for the apportionment of inheritances. It is possible that
Moslem history, geography, and a few elements of chem-
istry or alchemy may also have been taught in Fez in this
period. However, the natural and social sciences do not
appear to have held a large place in the school program of
Fez, even though there figured among the secretaries of

Abu'l-Hasan a certain Abu'l-'Abbas Ahmad ibn Shuayb, a physician and a remarkable botanist.

The essential character of all this instruction must be stressed. It was an instruction of transmission, whose conservative character is clearly marked. The primordial task of the doctors of Fez, as of their colleagues in the Moslem world and in medieval Europe, consisted of transmitting the truth, not a contingent truth painfully acquired by human experience, but divine truth, revealed to men through the intermediary of the Prophet Mohammed and clarified by the most erudite men of Islam. Their first duty was to deliver to their successors this truth intact, without subtracting anything from it or adding anything to it—hence the conservative character of their teaching. The qualities they sought to develop in their pupils were above all, therefore, memory and the strictest fidelity: they delivered to them a sacred trust which they, in their turn, would transmit without adulteration to their successors. This instruction is much more comparable to that of theological seminaries than of modern universities.

Courses were suspended two days a week, probably Thursdays and Fridays. On the other days, they began early in the morning, after the dawn prayer, and ended for the midafternoon prayer. Each teacher naturally had his own schedule and had to hold a certain number of sessions per week. He installed himself on a low platform, from which however he could dominate his pupils, who squatted around him flush with the floor. The course consisted of reading and commenting on the works of a more ancient author, often one of the classics of Islam, but preferably one of the classics of the Malikite school, which will be mentioned later on, and to which belonged, without exception, all the savants of Fez, and of North Africa in general. A pupil was requested to read; the master interrupted from time to time to give a more or less lengthy commentary on the passage which had just been read, or a sentence, or a single word which seemed to him to require explanation. Thus the teaching was primarily reading and commentary. It is not certain that the pupils took written notes, so highly trained was their memory.

Students were divided into two categories: those who were natives of the city itself and those who were not. The first-mentioned naturally continued to live with their families and their maintenance posed no problem. The others came from a few Moroccan cities or even from Tlemcen, since for some twenty years, beginning in 1337, Tlemcen formed part of the Marinide kingdom. But many also were natives of the country, some from the agricultural regions of the north, between Fez and the Mediterranean, some from the Atlantic plains, some from the Saharan regions, Tafilalet and other localities. It does not seem that, apart from rare exceptions, the mountain-dwelling Berbers studied in Fez, and there is a peremptory reason for this: they did not know Arabic and learned it only by accident. The majority of these "foreign" students were lodged in the *madrasas*. In principle these colleges offered a room to each student and in certain ones more than a hundred rooms had been constructed; they were cells, bare-walled and rather narrow, but which were considered an appreciable luxury by these boys accustomed to living in poor country houses and sometimes in tents in all seasons. It may be inferred that, as was the case later on, the afflux of students often caused a single room to be occupied by two, or even by three students, who were still comfortable there. Leo Africanus tells us that in the fourteenth century "each student was provided with supplies and clothing for seven years" out of the budget of the pious foundations. This bit of information, besides furnishing a valuable clue as to the average duration of studies, permits the inference that the *madrasas* had been richly endowed at the outset. In addition to the state subsidies, these students, at least the ones in more comfortable circumstances, received provisions from their families. The others found supplementary sources of income by participating in funeral services where they recited prayers, and perhaps giving lessons, as has been the custom of students in all times and places. In short, they do not seem to have been badly off; the Marinides had done much in their behalf. No chronicler tells us that they were particularly turbulent; the general atmosphere of Fez, with its respectability, and the quasi-monastic life they led, imposed upon them a sort of discipline that they do not appear to have violated; and then the state, or the pious foundations, which came practically to the same thing, gave them enough to exact responsible behavior on their part—in case of a prank, they ran the risk of dismissal.

There were several possibilities of employment for students native to Fez, once their studies were finished; they might enter state administration, which offered numerous openings, or else they became professors if their family connections facilitated matters for them, or again they set themselves up as notaries or lawyers, careers with promising future in this city fond of legal proceedings; others finally, after having acquired a good culture, returned to the business of their fathers or their families and contented themselves with managing the family inheritance. The "foreigners" returned for the most part to their town, their village, or their tribe of origin, to carry on there occupations of teaching or judicature. The most gifted of them could try to compete with the young men of Fez on their own ground and they succeeded at times: provided they made an advantageous marriage, they acquired rights of citizenship. We have no idea of the number of these students, nor of the size of the "graduating classes" which each year left the schools of Fez; they seem to have been rather exactly proportioned to the needs of the country, since at no moment do we find an indication of intellectual overproduction. The certain result of this instruction was that the Moroccan élite, at least the élite of the learned, received the same training. Whether it was a question of the world of business, administration, teaching, or judicature, all had been cast in the same conformist mould, all spoke the same intellectual language, and spread through the country the same truth, carefully transmitted from generation to generation. This offered positive benefits for the cohesion of the country, and probably contributed to the formation in certain regions of Morocco, in the Arabized and not the Berber regions, of what we would call in our modern idiom "a national consciousness." But this uniformity was not without its disadvantages; it stereotyped Moroccan culture, it constricted personalities, and perhaps it should be held responsible in the long run for the intellectual immobility that Morocco experienced for centuries. This was a culture that turned round upon itself.

The University was certainly the great intellectual center of Fez, but there was another—the court. All the chroniclers who describe this period in the history of Fez are in agreement in saying that Abu'l-Hasan and Abu'Inan were both scholarly princes, strongly interested in intellectual life. The traveler Ibn Batuta relates that the sovereign had the custom, when he was in his capital, of gathering around him each morning scholars and learned men and of conversing with them on a subject of study; either they read and construed before him a passage from the Koran or from the prophetic tradition, or they took as text of the discussion a work of law, or else they broached a work of mysticism. Poetry also received recognition at the court; Leo Africanus relates that the sovereign organized poetic competitions, particularly on the occasion of the celebration of the Prophet Mohammed's birthday. "The reciter," he writes, "stood on a very high platform. Then, following the judgment of competent persons, the king gave to the most highly esteemed poet one hundred pieces of gold, a horse, a female slave, and the garment that he was wearing. He had fifty pieces of gold given to all the others, so that all took leave of him with a reward." There is no doubt that the Marinide sovereigns of the fourteenth century also gave vigorous encouragement to historical research. It is not by chance that the historical school of Fez flourished at that period. Ibn Khaldun, man of genius, greatest historian of North Africa up to the present time, and founder of historical sociology, lived several years at the court of Fez; the great Granadine historian and vizier, Lisan al-din Ibn al-Khatib, found refuge there before being traitorously assassinated by the order of his former master, the King of Granada. The Marinide sovereigns of the fourteenth century had several official historiographers, among them Ibn Marzuq, who recounted the splendors of the reign of Abu'l-Hasan. It is characteristic, however, that philosophy had no place in this intellectual activity: the Marinide sovereigns did not have the breadth of view of their Almohade predecessors; their concept of intellectual life was guided by a strict and somewhat narrow orthodoxy which did not adjust to the boldness of an Ibn Tufayl or an Averrhoes, while the Almohade sovereigns of the end of the twelfth century did not hesitate to summon these great minds to their court.

Beside the authorized scholars and the writers who distinguished themselves in universally recognized genres, place must be made for the sharpshooters of intellectual life, those who employed genres dubious in the eyes of strict orthodoxy. Such were, first of all, the mystics. It has just been seen that Abu'Inan was interested in their works, but there is every reason to suppose that he granted status only to the most reasonable mystics, to those who added only a grain of love to orthodoxy. There were others more venturesome, more eccentric, and who certainly found no place in the entourage of the sovereign. Leo Africanus gives us, in regard to them, details which are not lacking in picturesqueness of a rather special nature: "It is not rare," he writes, "for some gentleman to invite to his festivities one of the masters among these principal Sufis (mystics) with all his disciples. When they arrive at the banquet, they begin by saying prayers and singing hymns. Once the meal is finished, the most aged begin to rend their garments and if, while dancing, one of these aged men falls, he is immediately raised up and set on foot again by one of the young Sufis, who frequently gives him a lascivious kiss. Whence has come the saying which is in the mouth of everyone in Fez: 'It is like the banquet of the hermits which made us become, from twenty, ten.' This means that, at night after the ball, each young disciple knows what awaits him." If credence is given to Leo Africanus, these mystics were therefore far from having irreproachable morals. But sometimes one must distrust this new convert to Christianity, who had a tendency to see in somber colors the civilization he had abandoned. Nevertheless, it may be admitted that at least on the intellectual and spiritual plane, there were in Fez anomalous persons who did not adhere to the ideals recognized by the community as a whole; this abode of conformity did shelter a few nonconformists. There were others beside the mystics, and certainly of lower stations: these were the possessors, or reputed to be such, of esoteric knowledge; perhaps they believed in their sorcery, but they also profited from public credulity. Consequently, underneath the doctrinal and moral rectitude proclaimed in Fez, there stirred, feebly perhaps, another type of humanity, a sort of society characterized by doubtful morals and devious intellectual procedures. We are inclined to grasp at the faint reassurance that this city, which wished to appear so respectable, was not entirely so, and suffered, as did the others, from weaknesses that were scarcely admitted, but which existed nonetheless. In spite of the rigid mold of the court and the university, there existed in fourteenth-century Fez a certain freedom of thought.

Let us not, however, be led astray by the picturesque and sometimes disquieting descriptions of Leo Africanus; this freedom of thought was highly limited and, in the over-all picture, intellectual life, however active it might be, was stereotyped and left little room for individual initiative and personality. Many chroniclers have garnished their accounts with poetic fragments of greater or lesser length. They all bear a strange resemblance to one another; they differ only in the arrangement and choice of words, but all carry a sort of identical trade-mark, rendering differentiation impossible. No one of them expresses a temperament. Whether one reads verse, rhymed prose, historical chronicles, or juridical treatises, the same general impression remains: culture, as conceived of in Fez, and in the whole Moslem world of the period, aimed at subjugating the personality, at making the individual the pure vehicle of a transcendent truth whose sole requisite was transmission intact. It required the intellectual power of an Ibn Khaldun to escape this collective pressure insistent that the cultivated man not be himself, but a sort of impersonal mannequin, acting and thinking like the whole group, not manifesting his own gifts except in a few infinitesimal and superficial details. Moreover it must be remembered that for a long period Ibn Khaldun did not enjoy great renown: the might of his genius astonished, scandalized perhaps, and found no echo in this society so impersonal in nature.

VII

RELIGIOUS LIFE

OWING TO ITS SHERIFIAN ORIGINS, Fez was immediately oriented not only toward commerce and life of the mind, but also (at least as much) toward spiritual life and piety. Well before the Marinides, it was one of the principal centers of Islam in Morocco. The endeavors of these sovereigns to give it additional luster in this domain have been mentioned; it is time now to undertake sketching a portrait of Fez, focus of Moslem life.

The rhythm of daily life was religious by its very nature. As could be observed in preceding chapters, the activity of artisans, merchants, scholars, and families was ordered by daily prayers, just as the annual alternations of work and leisure were governed by the liturgical calendar. It may be added that the language itself was profoundly, intimately marked by Islam. It is a pity that we do not have at our disposal texts which would give us an account of conversations taken from actual life in the period under consideration; it was unfortunately not the custom to transcribe everyday Arabic. But the literary texts which have come down to our time are garnished with religious expressions, and it may be asserted, without much risk of error, that a number of expressions still in use today in ordinary language have an ancient origin: the name of God and preoccupation with the supernatural occur in almost every sentence, not only in the language of the erudite, but also in the popular tongue. This phenomenon is certainly not peculiar to Fez: a religious orientation is most striking throughout the whole Moslem world, at least until our period. But it may be said that this religious orientation is particularly marked in Fez.

We know that Moslems are required, if at all possible, to assemble five times a day in the mosques, places where ritual purity is assured, to address in common the deity and to adore him above all else. Precise information is not available on the respect paid this religious observance in the fourteenth century. However, there is a trustworthy clue: the number of buildings pertaining to worship, according to the unanimous testimony of all our sources, was quite large. The first concern of the Marinides when they built their royal city of Fez Jdid was to construct there a mosque worthy of it; soon a *madrasa* and another mosque were to join the Great Mosque of this new city and, in the following century, two new mosques were to be erected in Fez Jdid, in proportion as the royal city developed. As for the old city, it was already well endowed with mosques and oratories; the Marinides however added two new mosques, the Shoemakers' Mosque and that of Abu'l-Hasan, and it must be remembered that all the *madrasas* included a prayer hall accessible not only to the students lodging there, but also to the faithful of the vicinity. If the mosques had not been much frequented, they would not have been constructed in such numbers, and the pious foundations set up for this purpose would not have been so numerous. It may therefore be affirmed without risk of error that the obligation of community prayer was respected by a high proportion of the men. The women, in effect, do not seem to have frequented these mosques much, for the enclosures reserved for women, such as may be seen in other Moslem countries, are rarely to be found here. This does not mean that the women of Fez were not pious; it is only an indication that their practices of piety took place at home.

It was the voice of the muezzin which, on every day that God made, ordered the day of the believer and brought him to the mosque of his choice at dawn, noon, midafternoon, sunset, and nightfall. However, it could happen that such and such a person found it physically impossible to repair to the mosque at the hour indicated. He could then make an individual prayer, in whatever spot he might find himself. All that was required was to lay out on the ground a length of cloth that he always carried with him: thus, established in a ritually pure space, he could address to his creator the act of adoration prescribed by the law. Each week, a particularly solemn prayer, that of Friday noon (this is why Friday is called in Arabic the day of the assembly), called together the faithful in the most important mosques. There the believers accomplished their ritual devotions and heard in addition a sermon, delivered by a regularly appointed preacher named by the sovereign upon the recommendation of the cadi. The preacher ascended into a mobile wooden pulpit, a work of art in the majority of cases, placed to the right of the niche, or *mihrab*, which indicated the direction of Mecca. From there he addressed the congregation, beginning by invoking the benediction of God on the Prophet, his family, his first successors, and the reigning sovereign. The Friday prayer thus took on the aspect of an act of political allegiance, renewed each week and particularly significant at the moment when a new sovereign came into power. Then the preacher addressed to his hearers a moral exhortation or a doctrinal explanation, according to his capabilities and also according to the circumstances. It will be seen further on that, on the occasion of the great Moslem festivals, solemn prayers were organized in the open air.

The second obligation of the Moslems, this an annual and not a daily one, is the fast of the month of Ramadan, the ninth month of the Mohammedan year. For a lunar month, that is to say during twenty-eight, twenty-nine, or thirty days, according to the date on which the crescent of the new moon can be observed at the beginning and end of Ramadan, the Moslem in the prime of life (children and old men are not subject to this obligation) must abstain from eating, from drinking, and from any sexual act between daybreak and nightfall, or, as it is expressed in the current speech, between the moment when it is possible to begin to distinguish a white thread from a black thread, and the moment when it is no longer possible to make a distinction between them. As the lunar year is eleven days shorter than the solar year, the month of Ramadan, which was originally an autumn month, falls therefore successively in all the seasons of the year, as well in full summer, when the heat is overwhelming and thirst excruciating, as in the dead of winter, when cold renders the lack of food even more painful. This is, then, a harsh ordeal in all periods, but particularly during the extreme seasons. There is every reason to think that in this city, where everyone was acquainted and all kept an eye on one another, the obligation of fasting was generally respected.

But the month of Ramadan, in Fez and in all North Africa, was not solely a great religious event; it was also a social event: for a whole month, the city changed rhythm. Meals took place the moment night fell, then during the evening, and finally toward the end of the night, but long enough before the stars fell, so as to be sure of not being surprised by daybreak while in the act of eating. And, in order that each one might be certain of not being late for this last nocturnal meal, a team of men circulated through the streets of the city, at an appropriate moment, and knocked on all doors to awaken the sleepers, not leaving any door until an answer had been obtained and the certainty that the household was wide awake—an indispensable precaution in a period when the alarm clock did not exist. A part of the night was thus spent in eating, but also in gathering in groups; Ramadan was the month for nocturnal receptions: visits were made to relatives and friends, and people retired very late. Consequently, during the whole morning, the city gave the impression of being deserted: the streets were almost empty, to the point where children could play there, which was not conceivable in normal times; shops and ateliers almost all remained closed, for people returned to bed after the dawn prayer, and enjoyed the satisfaction of an indispensable morning's sleep. It was only at the end of the morning that the city began to stir and resumed its activity, until the eagerly awaited hour for breaking the fast. In short, during this month, the normal activity of the city was greatly slowed down. This was a month of prayer and sacrifice, but also, to a certain extent, a month of relaxation and partial holiday. One night was particularly celebrated, the twenty-seventh, because it is traditionally considered as the one on which the Prophet received the first divine revelation. In order to commemorate this event, the Koran was recited in its entirety throughout the night, in the principal mosques of the city, by men who relieved each other at fixed intervals. In addition, according to popular belief, on that night God sent angels into all the regions inhabited by believers, and whoever thought he could distinguish one in the sky could make a prayer that had every chance of being granted. That is why it was called the Night of Destiny, *Laylat al-Qadr*. Consequently, the crowd spread through the streets, gazing ceaselessly toward the heavens with eyes illumined by faith. Finally, almost every evening of Ramadan, between the meal of breaking the fast and that which followed the nocturnal prayer, public courses were offered at least in the Mosque of the Kairwanians, and probably in several mosques of the city; they obviously treated religious subjects. This was therefore a sort of general retreat in which all classes of society participated for a whole month, a sort of annual bath of religious fervor.

This month of sacrifices and the canonical feast which immediately followed it furnished to the inhabitants of Fez, in addition, the opportunity for acquitting themselves of one of the fundamental obligations of the Moslem religion, the almsgiving ordained by the law. Originally, the alms had been conceived by Moslem society as a tax levied by the state and destined to relieve the misfortune of the poverty-stricken. In actual fact, this tax had quickly become one of the principal resources of the state, which naturally had need of a budget; the poor received from it only crumbs. This evolution may be confirmed throughout the whole of the Moslem world, in Morocco as elsewhere. The practice had then been established that, in addition to the tax so paid, the rich should periodically make gifts to the poor in their midst. In Fez at least, they did it during the month of Ramadan and on the occasion of the canonical festivals, in order that the poor might participate, in a humble measure, in the general rejoicing. These were gifts in cash, but also and perhaps chiefly, gifts in kind, and notably of food. Each well-to-do family in Fez had its regular poor who came on dates fixed by custom, not to beg for, but to receive as their due, the gifts that those favored by fortune had the strict obligation to bestow without stint. That was certainly not the sole reason for the absence of social disturbances in this city, but it was one of the reasons: the unfortunate did not have the impression of being set apart, of being considered as the "*damnés de la terre*," as would be shouted later on in a well-known revolutionary hymn; they knew that the rich not only gave them a portion of what God had bestowed on them, but also gave them their due, however slight it might be. They appear to have been content with it, since no indication permits us to affirm that there were social disturbances in Fez during the fourteenth century.

Each year took place the departure for the Pilgrimage (*hadj*) unless circumstances were extremely unfavorable, as for example, when war prevented the movement of caravans. There were individual departures, notably those of rich, bold men who did not hesitate to confront the risks of a sea voyage. Some pilgrims went to embark at Ceuta, at Badis, or at one of the ports which served Tlemcen, and in general took a Christian boat, Venetian, Genoese, Provençal, or Aragonese, for Egyptian or Syrian ships rarely called at these ports, and Maghrebian boats were few in number. Other pilgrims, the poorest ones, set out toward the east on foot; these spent several years in accomplishing the round trip, and without fail there were some who never returned. Still others set forth in private caravans. But the greatest number joined the official caravan which was organized each year, unless overcome by an insurmountable obstacle. This was a caravan all the more official in character since it often included one or more members, and at times even women, of the royal family. The preparations began several months in advance; the day of departure was a day of merrymaking throughout the city; people came to bid the fortunate travelers farewell, and many accompanied them during one stage, or even several stages, of their long journey toward the east. According to the political and climatic circumstances, the official caravan took different routes: either it proceeded not far from the coast, passing through Taza, Oujda, Tlemcen, Constantine, and Tunis, or else it skirted the foot of the Saharan Atlas, by way of Tafilalet, Figuig, Laghouat, Biskra, Tozeur, and Gabès. Frequently the return trips were individual, for some went on a pilgrimage to Jerusalem before returning to Fez. But, individual or collective, the returns were always celebrated with a flourish: people went out to meet the pilgrims, who had their arrival made known in advance, and accompanied them to the threshold of their dwellings. For several days after their return, they entertained the relatives and friends who came to congratulate them and to receive their share of the divine grace which the pilgrims brought back from the "House of Allah." Naturally no statistics are available on the pilgrimage in the fourteenth century; it may be assumed, however, that the pilgrims were not numerous: the risks and the length of the trip and the magnitude of the expenses to be undertaken made of this a veritable ordeal, reserved for a small number of wealthy and courageous men. Nevertheless, we have proof that several notables of Fez accomplished the pilgrimage at least twice in their lives, and we have mentioned that the number of pilgrims was sufficient to create a far from negligible stream of trade between Fez and the countries of the Moslem East. This indicates that it was a flourishing institution and furnishes an appreciable means for measuring the piety of the city.

Each year there also took place several religious festivals in which the whole population participated. There was first the festival of the breaking of the fast, or Little Festival, which was celebrated on the first day of the month which followed Ramadan. This was, like all the others, a movable feast, since it was linked to the lunar calendar. If the weather was favorable, the festival was marked first of all, during the morning, by a great prayer in the open air. No mosque, in fact, was vast enough to contain the whole masculine population of Fez and the representatives of the tribes round about who assembled on this occasion. The ceremony was held in a traditional spot, to the northwest of the old city, in the vicinity of the Gate of the Burned Man. A little white wall marked the direction for prayer and mats furnished by the administration of religious properties covered the ground, so that believers could accomplish their devotions on a ritually pure soil. Early in the morning the crowd gathered in great numbers: citizens dressed in their best finery, horsemen from the neighboring tribes on beautifully caparisoned horses. The sovereign, or his representative if the sovereign was not in Fez, arrived in a great procession, surrounded by armed soldiers and dignitaries clothed in white. He conducted the prayer himself and heard a sermon appropriate to the occasion, delivered by the royal preacher. Then, the religious ceremony over, the sovereign passed in front of the horsemen of the tribes, grouped around their standards, and received successively their homage. During this time, the women of Fez were bustling about in their homes preparing the noon meal, the first of its sort for a month.

The day was spent in feasting and receptions, as were the following days, but to a lesser degree; in fact the traditional duration of the festival was seven days, but the majority of the inhabitants of Fez resumed their normal activity at the end of two or three days, remaining idle again on the seventh day.

The second festival, seventy days after the preceding one, that is to say the tenth day of the last month of the Mohammedan year, was the feast of the sacrifice, or Great Festival. This was the day on which took place near Mecca the most important ceremony of the pilgrimage, the sacrificing of a sheep, which commemorated Abraham's sacrifice. Those who did not have the good fortune to participate in this immolation on the very spot where it had occurred many centuries before participated in it by making their own sacrifice of a sheep per family. Many weeks earlier the country people of the vicinity were bringing sheep to the Thursday Market, and the sale took place every day during the week which preceded the festival; all those who were able considered it a point of honor to acquire for the occasion a handsome sheep and to fatten it at home so that it would be in proper condition at the desired moment. The poorer people contented themselves with a kid or shared the purchase of an animal with neighbors equally lacking in means. The day of the feast itself began with a prayer in the open air, analogous to that of the Little Festival, with the difference that, once the prayer was finished, the sovereign with his own hand cut the throat of a handsome sheep, which was borne still gasping to the dwelling of the cadi of the city by a cavalcade of porters mounted on horses. If the victim arrived at the destination still alive, this was a fortunate omen for the coming year. As soon as the ceremony was over, the citizens hastened to return home to proceed in their turn with the immolation of their own sheep. It was customary to offer the best morsels of the victim to persons to whom one desired to express friendship or respect. Like the preceding one, this festival was the occasion for general idleness and numerous receptions.

The third festival, in chronological order, fell on the tenth day of the first month of the new year, whence its name of *'Ashura* (the Arabic root *'ashara* means ten). This was a traditional, not a canonical, festival and the reason for this will be understood when it is apparent that it was composed of disparate elements, many of which were certainly of pre-Islamic origin. The purely religious element is probably of Shi'ite origin, since it is a question of the commemoration of the death of Husayn, grandson of the Prophet, who died a martyr's death in 680 at Kerbela (Iraq). Popular tradition of Fez chose to commemorate also on that day the death of Fatima, daughter of the Prophet, of which the exact date is not known, and even the death of the Prophet himself, who in reality yielded up his soul on the 13 *Rabi'al-awwal*, 9 (June 8, 632). This was therefore in principle a day, and even a month, of mourning: in fact, during this whole month of Muharram, the professional musicians of Fez abstained from making use of their instruments. But it was at the same time a joyous festival, when gifts were distributed to the children. Popular tradition in Fez explained this contradiction by relating that at the moment when the Prophet was at the point of death, the children of the house had begun to weep and they had been given toys to console them, or else that the same thing had been done for the children of Husayn on the day of their father's death. However this might be, the children of Fez were not at all sad on

the day of 'Ashura. In the Koranic schools, the night preceding the festival was brilliantly illuminated by tapers
burning in the classrooms. As soon as day broke, and before the children returned home, the schoolmaster made
them learn a short lesson in order to begin the year auspi-
ciously. Likewise the artisans went to work at their stalls
and the merchants at their shops for a moment during the
morning, so that the new year might be a prosperous one
for them. In the houses, doors, windows, wardrobes, and
chests were thrown open, so that the divine benediction
could penetrate without hindrance into the innermost re-
cesses of the dwelling. Finally, the men had their heads
shaved, all trimmed their nails, and put on new clothing
that day. All these practices are rites of renewal which
have no direct connection with the Moslem religion, and
which are quite probably deeply rooted in ancient Berber
beliefs. Did the custom of playing the tabor on the day
of 'Ashura already exist in the time of the Marinides, as
was the case later on? Nothing permits us to affirm it, nor
to deny it either. It is certain in any case that the 'Ashura,
although a festival more than semiprofane, was celebrated
with enthusiasm in Fez, but the festivities were of shorter
duration than for the preceding festivals.

The fourth festival celebrated the anniversary of the
birth of the Prophet (*al-Mawlid*, pronounced *Mulud* in
Morocco), the twelfth day of the third month of the Mohammedan year (*Rabīʾ al-awwal*). This festival had been
made official by the Marinide Sultan Abu Yaʾqub in the
year 1292. It consisted primarily of a prayer vigil, during
the night which preceded the anniversary day; panegyrics
were pronounced, in prose or in verse. It has been seen
previously that the Marinide sovereign organized each
year on this occasion a poetic competition whose subject

was quite naturally a eulogy of the envoy of God. For seven days, at least in theory, receptions and festivities succeeded one another, the first and the seventh being the days of greatest celebration.

These great festivals eclipsed the others, but others did exist: the patronal feasts of the most venerated saints, which all had the same character, at once social and religious, quite like the principal festivals. In addition, there occurred at times exceptional ceremonies, such as the prayers to obtain rain. The Moslem ritual provides in fact a special prayer, in which the whole masculine population takes part, when drought is prolonged and crops are endangered. It is probable that in the fourteenth century, as in our time, this perfectly orthodox prayer was accompanied by rites of sympathetic magic, at least in the humble and ignorant strata of the population. It is probable also that formerly, as today, a few feasts of clearly pre-Islamic character were interspersed among the manifestations of orthodox piety. Thus it was that on the first of January of the Julian calendar, always observed in the rural regions of Morocco by the farmers, took place the festival of *Haguza*, a festival primarily gastronomic: for four days all those who were able feasted—pancakes were particularly enjoyed on this occasion. At the beginning of July, the festival of *Ansra* was celebrated: for a whole day people vied in sprinkling one another with water in the streets and on the terraces, for the women took an active part in the festivity.

These deviations, or rather these survivals from a distant past anterior to Islam do not conflict with the assertion that, all things considered, Fez was a pious city and one of satisfactory orthodoxy. For a long time, certainly since the Almoravides and quite likely even before them, the city had submitted, as had all the rest of North Africa, to the rules of one of the four juridical schools recognized as orthodox by all the doctors of the law, that of the imam Malik, a Medinan of the end of the eighth century. This was a strict and formalistic school which had little by little moulded in its image Moslem observance in Fez. The hazards of history had probably been an element in this adherence, but figuring in it also was a certain Berber austerity which manifested itself throughout the whole history of North Africa and adapted well to the minute and precise regulations of the Malikite school. However, it has been noted here and there, in Fez as elsewhere, that a local custom would superimpose itself upon the law, as it was interpreted by the Malikite doctors. This custom was not in contradiction to the law, but rendered it more specific on certain points of detail and suggested the options open to the people of Fez when by chance the Malikite doctrine left the believers a certain freedom of choice. The doctors of Fez had therefore no feeling of transgressing orthodoxy when they gave the custom a place beside the former. And from the moment the doctors were of this opinion no one contradicted them, for they were the great masters in religious matters, the arbiters to whom people had recourse in case of doubt or discussion, and whose decision was complied with unquestioningly because they were considered to be not only scholars, but repositories of the truth. They were therefore the regulators of religious life in Fez and they were conscious of it. They had a lofty idea of their importance and of their knowledge, but also of their responsibilities. The sovereign himself consulted them as soon as orthodoxy appeared to him to be in question, and he bowed before their verdict. If they were conscious of the importance of their role, they also knew its limits and took no hand in politics. It is curious to ascertain that in this society, where in principle the spiritual and the temporal were inextricably bound up with each other, the repositories of the truth did not venture into the political domain and practiced in actual fact the separation of powers, to which they were not held legally, far more strictly than did their contemporaries, the bishops of Christian Europe.

However, the official representatives of Malikite orthodoxy were not quite the sole directors of piety in Fez. They had to reckon, to a certain extent, with the mystics, the saints living or dead, who exercised perhaps less influence than they did on the minds of the citizens, but who ruled them through the emotions. The fact is that orthodox piety was not without a certain dryness: it was distressingly legalistic and did not always satisfy—far from it—the needs for sentimental effusion, for personal attachment, that many human hearts demanded. The mystics were there to satisfy these demands. Without any doubt, there were charlatans and eccentrics among them; but there is no doubt either that their number included many sincere believers who, not contenting themselves with the fear of God and the sentiment of his all-powerfulness, experienced the need of loving him, and of quite frankly offering him their hearts. Nevertheless, the mysticism of Fez, as well as we are able to judge, remained within reasonable limits and in no way endangered orthodoxy.

The manifestations of collective piety mentioned earlier are the unquestionable testimony of a unanimous transport toward divinity. But leaving aside these ceremonies which occupied a large place in the lives of the inhabitants of Fez, acts of individual piety should be considered—acts which can, better than any other indication, give an idea of the spiritual temper of a human group, for they do not admit of automatism, of soulless imitation, inherent in all collective action. Anyone living in Fez cannot fail to be impressed by the atmosphere of piety that is breathed there: the idea of God is everywhere present, in the smallest acts of life, from the set phrases of polite manners to the aphorisms borrowed from the Koran or the Prophetic Tradition, which form the backdrop of polite conversations. Is a merchant awaiting customers? He tells his beads, reciting pious phrases, or reads an edifying book. At any hour of the day, the faithful are to be seen entering the sanctuaries—the most celebrated people as well as the most humble—in order to place themselves, though it be only for an instant, in the presence of God. That pure conformism exists here and there, that the inhabitants of Fez are no better than the common run of men, should not be surprising to anyone. But this cannot alter the impression of profound and general piety which Fez emits. It is a stable and simple piety, without ostentatious gestures, without excessive transports, an easy propensity—grown almost natural—for communication with the supernatural world. In the hagiographic collections are found notations in the manner of the following: "Often in the middle of the night, he left his house and proceeded to the bath to perform his ablutions there. Then he went to accomplish his devotions and returned home."

In addition, from the founding of the city up to the Marinide era, and even to our day, Fez discloses no trace of heresy or dogmatic deviations terminating in upheavals of any size. The religious life of this city has developed under the sign of serenity, apart from the doubt and discords experienced by other regions of the Moslem world. This is doubtless explained by the fact that, in the religious domain as in the others, the people of Fez have not swerved from their natural moderation. There is among them no great mystic, such as al-Hallaj, no religious reformer such as an Ibn Tumart, who endeavors to impose an absolute doctrine upon an entire population. It is a fervent, vigorous piety, common to all, not at all incapable of mystical transports, but above everything else "human, tractable," more remarkable by its continuity, by its evenness, than by its paroxysms, and tolerant not only of followers of other religions (it must not be forgotten that, according to tradition, the great Jewish scholar Maimonides taught at the Mosque of the Kairwanians), but also of the diverse tendencies of Maghrebian Islam, considering with the same benevolence the mystics and the gentle visionaries, the ritualistic Malikites, the adepts in the worship of the saints, and the populace attached by ignorance to ancient beliefs just barely covered over, as if for modesty's sake, by a slight Islamic veil. The important thing, in the eyes of the majority, is that each day, almost at each hour, thousands of spirits affirm their belief in the One God and that, from the innumerable sanctuaries of Fez, rises unceasingly, with an accent of conviction, a symphony of praises addressed to the Most High, in which each one, according to his abilities, plays his part with the same faith.

CONCLUSION

For two more centuries, Fez was to remain the capital of the Marinides and to preserve its relative opulence and its equilibrium; then, in the middle of the sixteenth century, the Sa'adians would become masters of Morocco and, as men of the south, would make Marrakech their capital. Fez would, however, continue to be their second city; the Sa'adian sultans would sojourn there frequently, would embellish it, and would always maintain there a governor chosen from the nearest relatives of the sovereign. But, at the beginning of the seventeenth century, when Morocco was to founder in anarchy, Fez would suffer cruelly; its economy would be sharply affected, civil war would tear it apart; it would lose population sharply, and this unhappy period would endure for more than fifty years. When in 1666 the first Alawite sovereign, Mawlay al-Rashid, was to seize the city and attempt to revive its economy, hope would return to the hearts of the inhabitants of Fez, but not for long: Mawlay Isma'il, who was to succeed his brother in 1672, would feel only aversion for Idris's city and would establish his capital at Meknes, losing no opportunity to persecute the inhabitants of Fez. Then would come the anarchy of the second third of the eighteenth century, during which Fez would be under the perpetual menace of Berber tribes or the troops of the various pretenders to the throne. The city would not breathe freely again until around 1760, when the wise and able Sidi Mohammad would succeed in restoring order to his kingdom. But at that time Fez would regain only a diminished equilibrium, because it would be the capital of a country arrested in its development and set apart from the rhythm of the world.

Can it be said that the French Protectorate and its consequences drew Fez out of its semi-lethargy? Yes, to a certain extent, if it is taken into consideration that the merchants of Fez have flocked into all the other important economic centers of Morocco, that the middle class of Fez has had, since Moroccan independence, a large share in the government of the country, either through the intermediary of ministers and leaders of the principal political parties, or through the medium of functionaries that Idris's city furnishes in great numbers in consequence of its long tradition of culture. But if Fez participates actively in modern Moroccan life it is, notwithstanding, only a provincial city. The seat of government was fixed at Rabat by General Lyautey, has remained there up to the present, and seems to be taking deeper and deeper root. The great commercial center is at Casablanca. Rabat already shelters the modern intellectual center of Morocco: the budding Moroccan University is established there. All this makes the future of Fez appear limited, leaves it with scarcely more than its past, its old Moslem university whose fate is uncertain, its modern seats of learning, which will probably justify the creation of branches of the Moroccan University, if the latter develops as anticipated. Like all the other Moroccan cities, Fez has seen its population increase, but in smaller measure than Casablanca, Rabat, or even Marrakech; it is no longer, from the economic point of view, more than a secondary city, active without any doubt because the surrounding region is relatively prosperous, destined probably for an industrial future, notably as regards the processing of leathers and wools, but dependent upon Casablanca and isolated from the vast mining enterprises which constitute the great wealth of modern Morocco. It is therefore permissible to conclude that, except in the event of an unforeseeable reversal, the fourteenth century is indeed the moment when Fez reached its fullest fruition.

It has been seen that, even at that period, the impetus and the refulgence of the city were limited. In a diminished Moslem world, as was the case at the time, Fez was able to fill the role of a great Moslem capital; but by reading what precedes it can be seen that its intellectual influence scarcely transcended the boundaries of Morocco, and that the city's economic relations went but little further. It did not experience the rapid and brilliant development of cities such as Cairo and Baghdad, to mention only Moslem cities; it suffered from its isolation at a time when the Atlantic Ocean did not exist for human commerce; it suffered also from historic circumstances which prevented it from establishing relations, which would probably have been fruitful, with the Iberian Peninsula and with Western Europe.

However, it merits the renown which has been ascribed to it, because it was able to bring into flower within its walls a genuine civilization; it knew how to fashion for itself an art of living to which it has remained faithful up to the present and whose primary constituent is stability. A reasonable city, where the inhabitants have been accustomed to look at facts in their true light and draw from them what they may yield, without ever seeking the impossible. A stable city, where commerce and money count for a great deal, but are not everything; where the artisan, the worker in general, feel themselves respected and are not ashamed of their modest situations in life; where the life of the mind fortunately counterbalances the desire for gain; where religious feeling is intense and deep, but does not turn to excess, to persecution and vicious strife; where the court itself has never crushed the city with its importance and its majesty. Fez is not, as has often been said, the city of mystery, but the city of good sense and good living. This is probably its principal merit and it is a quality deservedly great.

SELECTED BIBLIOGRAPHY

Ibn Abi Zar'al-Fasi. *Kitab al-anis al-mutrib bi-rawd al-qirtas fi akhbar muluk al-Maghrib wa-tarikh madinat Fas*. Text edited by Tornberg (Upsala, 1843). Translated by the same into Latin, under the title *Annales regum Mauritaniæ* (Upsala, 1846) and into French by Beaumier, under the title *Histoire des souverains du Maghreb et Annales de la ville de Fès* (Paris, 1860). This work was written in the first third of the fourteenth century.

Abu'l-Hasan 'Ali al-Jaznaï, *Zahrat al-as*. Edited and translated by A. Bel. Algiers, 1923. A work dating from the first half of the fourteenth century.

Johannes Leo Africanus. *Description de l'Afrique*. Translated by A. Epaulard. 2 vols., Paris, 1956. A work written in the first third of the sixteenth century. The description of Fez occupies an important place in it.

Ibn al-Qadi. *Jadhwat al-iqtibas fi man hall min al-'alam madinat Fas*. Lithographed in Fez, A. H. 1309. A work of the first half of the seventeenth century.

Muhammad b. Jáfar al-Kattani. *Al-azhar al-'atirat al-anfas bi-dhikr ba'd mahasin qutb al-Maghrib wa-taj madinat Fas*. Lithographed in Fez, A. H. 1314.

———. *Salwat al-anfas wa-muhadhatat al-aqyas bi-man uqbira min al-'ulama wa's-sulaha bi-Fas*. 3 vols., lithographed in Fez, A. H. 1316.

Selected Bibliography

Aubin, Eugène. *Le Maroc d'aujourd'hui*. Paris, 1904.

Gaillard, Henri. *Une ville d'Islam: Fez*. Paris, 1905.

Tharaud, Jean et Jérôme. *Fez ou les Bourgeois de l'Islam*. Paris, 1930.

Le Tourneau, Roger. *Fès avant le Protectorat*. Casablanca, 1949.

INDEX

Index

The Centers of Civilization Series, of which this volume is the fourth, is intended to include accounts of the great cities of the world during particular periods of their flowering, from ancient times to the present. The following list is complete as of the date of publication of this volume:

1. Charles Alexander Robinson, Jr. *Athens in the Age of Pericles.*
2. Arthur J. Arberry. *Shiraz: Persian City of Saints and Poets.*
3. Glanville Downey. *Constantinople in the Age of Justinian.*
4. Roger Le Tourneau. *Fez in the Age of the Marinides.*